How to think like
STEVE JOBS

How to think like
STEVE JOBS

DANIEL SMITH

Michael O'Mara Books Limited

First published in Great Britain in 2013 by
Michael O'Mara Books Limited
9 Lion Yard
Tremadoc Road
London SW4 7NQ

A CIP catalogue record for this book is available from the British Library.

Papers used by Michael O'Mara Books Limited are natural,
recyclable products made from wood grown in sustainable forests.
The manufacturing processes conform to the environmental
regulations of the country of origin.

ISBN: 978-1-78243-068-1 in hardback print format
ISBN: 978-1-78243-188-6 in paperback print format
ISBN: 978-1-78243-085-8 in ePub format
ISBN: 978-1-78243-086-5 in Mobipocket format

1 2 3 4 5 6 7 8 9 10

www.mombooks.com

Cover design by Greg Stevenson
Designed and typeset by Envy Design Ltd
Printed and bound by CPI Group (UK) Ltd,
Croydon CR0 4YY

For Rosie

Contents

Introduction

When Steve Jobs died from complications related to pancreatic cancer on 5 October 2011, the news was received with an outpouring of grief unprecedented in the history of industry and commerce. It was the lead item on television and radio news channels around the world. It filled the front pages of countless newspapers and magazines and trended on Twitter. Tributes were left in extraordinary numbers on internet forums and social networking sites; there were 35 million online tributes from China alone. Leading figures from the worlds of politics, business and entertainment issued statements mourning his passing and celebrating his remarkable life. It was the sort of response usually reserved for cultural icons such as Princess Diana, or for the most beloved stars of music, stage and screen. Yet it was not so surprising that Jobs evoked such a response, for his businesses impacted – and continue to do so – on all of our lives.

You do not need to be a Mac user, iPod addict or disciple of the iPhone for his life's work to affect you. It is not too strong to say that none of those institutions mentioned above – the news media, the entertainment world, the internet, politics or business – would exist in the forms that they do today without his influence. For he not only equipped each of these sectors with tools that changed the way they work, but also altered society's attitudes on how we relate to technology and how we seek to do business. One trending tweet summarized how the world had been defined by three apples: 'The one that Eve ate, the one that dropped on Newton's head and the one that Steve built.'

'There may be no greater tribute to Steve's success than the fact that much of the world learned of his passing on a device he invented.'

BARACK OBAMA

What was most remarkable about the tributes paid to Jobs was how millions of people who had never come into personal contact with him felt a genuine bond. They were all members of

Team Jobs, each with a slightly different take on what he had represented. For some he was quite simply a genius: an inventor, innovator, boundary-pusher and visionary. A maverick. For others he was an inspiration: a man who could spot a good idea, tweak it to greatness and then sell it with unparalleled success. A sort of P. T. Barnum figure for the modern world, cropping up at intervals with the latest 'greatest gizmo on earth', which he successfully persuaded us we just had to have.

To those rather less enamoured of him, Steve Jobs was a bully, an icon of consumerism and a plagiarist. All of these views have at least some legitimacy. If he was a great man, he wasn't necessarily always a good one. What is beyond doubt, though, is that he was a genuine one-off.

With Steve Wozniak, he revolutionized the personal computer business. That alone would have been enough to secure him a sizeable footnote in twentieth-century history. In truth, for a while it looked as if that would indeed be his great contribution. But then he got his second wind: from the mid-1990s he transformed animated cinema and the film industry in general by giving Pixar its wings. Then, as the old century faded and a new one bloomed, he oversaw a period of almost miraculous creativity at Apple. The iMac rejuvenated the PC world, and was soon followed in short order by the iPod, which turned the music business on its head, the iPad – which has, among other achievements, underpinned a change in the way we read that was all but unthinkable ten years ago – and the iPhone, which, for many of its owners, has come to represent an entire 'life in a pocket'.

Over the course of his remarkable career, arguably Jobs' greatest achievement was to turn the essentially nerdy into something stylish and sexy. He addressed the geek in each of us and made us feel as if we were imbued instead with the spirit of Ned Kelly. He also understood that, by embracing innovation, he would get some things wrong along the way. Even as the arch perfectionist, he accepted this as long as every bit of knowledge was wrung from the experience to ensure better results next time. In his own words: 'Sometimes when you innovate, you make mistakes. It is best to admit them quickly, and get on with improving your other innovations.'

Underlying all Jobs' work was a belief in getting the simple things right. Of course, he realized that products need a visceral appeal, as evidenced by his comments to *Fortune Magazine* in 2000: 'We made the buttons on the screen look so good you'll want to lick them.' But he also knew that you can make a product as sleek and irresistible-looking as you like and it will all be for nothing if it doesn't do the job. As he said in 2003: 'It's not just what it looks like and feels like. Design is how it works.'

As the creator of era-defining must-have products, Steve Jobs was not merely a rule-breaker with the Midas touch but rather someone who rewrote the entire rule book. He was a man who was intent on making, in his own words, 'a dent in the universe'. By that reckoning, he was a phenomenal success. So let us take a look at both what he said and what he did – frequently admirable but sometimes less so – and begin our journey inside the mind of this remarkable figure.

Timeline of a Remarkable Life

1955   Steve Jobs is born and adopted by Paul and Clara Jobs.

1971   Jobs is introduced to Steve 'Woz' Wozniak.

1976   Apple is founded and the Apple I is exhibited for the first time.

1977   The Apple II is launched.

1978   Jobs' girlfriend, Chrisann Brennan, gives birth to a daughter, Lisa.

1980   Apple becomes a public company and is valued at $1.78 billion.

1982   *Time* magazine names the personal computer as 'Machine of the Year' and singles out Jobs as the man 'who kicked the door open and let the personal computer move in'.

1984 The Apple Macintosh is launched.

1985 Jobs leaves Apple and sets up NeXT.

1986 Jobs buys The Graphics Group from George Lucas. The company is later renamed Pixar.

1987 Steve Wozniak leaves full-time employment with Apple to pursue other interests.

1988 NeXT debuts its first computer.

1989 Pixar's *Tin Toy* wins an Oscar for Best Animated Short.

1990 Jobs marries Laurene Powell.

1991 Powell gives birth to a son, Reed.

1995 Pixar releases *Toy Story*, which receives a Special Achievement Oscar and earns almost $200 million in the US alone. Powell gives birth to a daughter, Erin.

1996 Apple buys NeXT and Jobs becomes a consultant to the Apple Board.

1997 Jobs returns to Apple and becomes Interim Chief Executive Officer.

1998 Powell gives birth to a daughter, Eve.

2000 Jobs announces that he is to be Apple's CEO on a permanent basis.

2001 The first Apple Stores open and the iPod is launched.

2002 Pixar's *Monsters Inc.* wins an Oscar for Best Original Song.

Timeline

2003 The iTunes Music Store is launched.

2004 Jobs receives treatment for pancreatic cancer. Pixar's *Finding Nemo* wins an Oscar for Best Animated Film.

2005 Pixar's *The Incredibles* wins Oscars for Best Animated Feature Film and Best Sound Editing.

2006 Pixar is bought by Disney, with Jobs gaining a place on the Disney board. Apple launches the MacBook.

2007 Apple Computer Inc. is rebranded as Apple Inc. The iPhone is launched.

2008 The MacBook Air is launched. Pixar's *Ratatouille* wins the Best Animated Film Oscar.

2009 Jobs announces he is taking a six-month leave of absence to resolve his health issues. *Fortune* magazine names him CEO of the decade. Pixar's *WALL-E* wins an Oscar for Best Animated Feature.

2010 The iPad is launched. Apple achieves sales of $65 billion, with profits of $14 billion. It overtakes Microsoft as the world's most valuable technology company. Pixar's *Up* wins Oscars for Best Animated Feature and Best Original Score.

2011   Apple is valued at $376 billion, briefly becoming the world's most valuable firm. Pixar's *Toy Story III* wins Oscars for Best Animated Feature and Best Original Song. It becomes the highest-grossing animated movie of all time, bringing in over $1 billion worldwide. On 24 August, Jobs resigns as Apple's CEO. On 5 October he passes away.

Get to the Top

Be an Outsider

'I will only eat leaves picked by virgins
in the moonlight.'

STEVE JOBS

For a man who attained enormous wealth and stood astride the corporate world, Steve Jobs did a remarkably good job to avoid becoming just another rich, white, middle-aged man in a suit and tie. He had an uncanny knack of persuading his customers that they were not merely filling the coffers of a huge multinational. Instead, he persuaded us that, by buying Apple, we were taking a step towards asserting our own individuality and creativity. The message seemed to be: Join Team Jobs and join an army of outsiders breaking down walls.

So how did he do it? Quite simply, because Steve Jobs truly believed that an outsider was just what he was.

A bumpy start

From the moment of his birth on 24 February 1955, Steve Jobs found himself cut adrift from the path of normality. His Syrian-born father, John Jandali, and his fresh-faced mother, Joanne Schieble, were both students. Joanne's father was far from impressed with her romantic dalliances and so it was that her new baby was immediately put up for adoption – only for the intended adoptive parents to pull out of the undertaking. Steve thus came to be taken in by Clara and Paul Jobs, a sweet couple of limited means but with a vast wealth of love to give.

A stroke of luck

If Steve had had a bumpy start to life, finding himself with the Jobs was his first great stroke of luck. They were intent on doing what was best for their young charge, notably planning for his college future despite neither of them having benefitted from such an opportunity themselves. As well as scrimping and saving to set up a college fund, Paul Jobs also passed on to Steve a serious passion for gadgets, gizmos and machines of all types. An avid car fan, Paul spent much of his spare time fixing up old vehicles and then selling them on. When Steve was old enough his father began to educate him in the skills required to take a machine apart and put it back together again, little knowing how invaluable this would prove.

Education

Steve's domestic life was relatively stable but he cultivated his outsider status away from home. Though a bright spark, he consistently had disciplinary problems at school. On one occasion, for instance, he planned to unfurl for a graduating class a banner – which he had helpfully signed – bearing a not-entirely-complementary hand signal. As he hit puberty his sense of not belonging only increased, and he evolved into a straggly-haired and angsty teen – a not uncommon phenomenon but one which Steve carried with him into his college years.

Having stretched his parents' resources to the extreme in order to get a place at Reed College in Portland, Oregon – a school renowned for its liberal arts syllabus – he gained a reputation among fellow students as something of a campus freak. He threw himself into the counterculture that took hold of American society in the late 1960s and early 1970s, experimenting with drugs, exploring his spiritual side and spending time working on what was effectively a communal apple orchard. He ultimately dropped out of college.

Experimentation

Jobs read books on diet that inspired him to follow a fruitarian regime – a form of extreme veganism that allows for a menu consisting only of fruits, nuts, seeds and so on. Prone to a certain level of food faddism throughout his life – he would later self-effacingly tell his biographer, Walter Isaacson, that 'I will only eat leaves picked by virgins in the moonlight' – he spent periods eating only one particular type of food, such as apples or carrots. At other times he went in for purging and also for fasting.

Jobs even believed that his diet helped keep his body odour at bay, but alas it did not – a fact that his work colleagues would have to bring to his attention in the early stages of his career.

The corporate ladder

Even when he entered corporate life at Atari, Jobs remained a law unto himself. Apart from the malodorous atmosphere he often left behind, he also refused to groom his long locks and was initially in the habit of wandering around the office in the most casual attire and usually with bare feet. Indeed, he later cost Apple at least one early investment deal when he turned up for a meeting and promptly put his uncovered extremities up on the desk of the man he was there to talk turkey with. He also cultivated a taste for ad hoc foot spas, which involved sticking his feet in the toilet pan and pulling the flush.

So the reason that Jobs could portray himself as apart from 'the Man' was because he was just that. Until his dying day, he retained a heartfelt belief that he was on the outside and it was from this position that he was able to develop his unique view of things. It is not necessary to gorge on berries or dodge deodorant to qualify as an outsider, but in a world where the pressure is generally on to fit in with the crowd, Jobs' life offers an object lesson in the advantages of embracing your outsider status.

Follow Your Own Road

'Your time is limited, so don't waste it living someone else's life. Don't let the noise of others' opinions drown out your own inner voice. And most important, have the courage to follow your heart and intuition.'

STEVE JOBS

His sense of standing apart from the mainstream resulted in Jobs developing a bespoke life philosophy of his own. While some of the eccentricities of his youth (and, in a few instances, of later life, too) can appear to the onlooker as wilfully outré and even a little self-indulgent, his willingness to embrace new and countercultural ideas would stand him in good stead throughout his professional life. His sense of outsider-dom allowed him the space to think freely and unconventionally.

Jobs' choice of Reed College was telling. Not for him the path many of his contemporaries took into the University of California or to a cheaper public college. Despite the strain it put upon his parents' finances – parents, let us remember, who had vowed to see him into college – he was determined to attend Reed with its reputation for free-wheelers and independent thinkers.

There he set about trying to discern just who he

was. He began dabbling in the mind-altering drug LSD, something he would later say was one of the defining experiences of his life. He sat around with his friends, trying to get at the 'truth of life' and evolving into a classic anti-Vietnam War, Dylan-loving hippie with a taste for books from the 'Mind, Body, Spirit' genre, especially anything claiming to reveal the secrets of Zen Buddhism.

Perhaps predictably, this lifestyle took its toll on Jobs' grades and he dropped out at the end of his first semester. It must have been hard on his parents and surely picked at the self-confidence of Jobs, who had asked so much of them in order to attend in the first place. It would prove to be an important step along his journey into adulthood, however, as was his next escapade: a backpacking trip around India.

The trip, a large part of which he undertook with a college friend, proved a true rite of passage. Jobs cut off his hair, found himself afflicted with severe stomach problems, met a guru or two and had an absolute whale of a time. After a few months he returned to California. He may not have 'found himself' but the intensity of the experience reinforced ideas widely explored in the Zen Buddhism literature that he had been reading; in Jobs' own words, he learned 'the power of intuition and experiential wisdom'.

That is to say, in accordance with Zen teaching, he increasingly valued personal experience over intellectual understanding.

This willingness to follow his gut feeling when others might rationally have chosen another path would be instrumental in setting him apart in the competitive technology market in years to come.

'Steve was among the greatest of American innovators – brave enough to think differently, bold enough to believe he could change the world, and talented enough to do it.'

BARACK OBAMA

A peek at Jobs' bookshelf provides significant insight into his inspirations and personal philosophy. He was certainly a broad reader. Plato, for instance, was a lifelong favourite, Jobs perhaps attracted to one of the founding fathers of Western philosophy by his shared passion for both the arts and the sciences.

Other classics included William Shakespeare's *King Lear,* which offers a vivid depiction of what can go wrong if you lose your grip on your empire, a story surely fascinating to any aspiring CEO. He was also a fan of Herman Melville's *Moby Dick,* arguably the greatest examination of the human soul in American literature. The poetry of Dylan Thomas, meanwhile, drew him in with its striking new forms and unerringly popular touch. He may also have enjoyed Thomas's reputation for rambunctiousness earned the hard way over a series of literary tours in the United States.

Here are a selection of other key works Jobs is known to have read:

- ▷ *Diet for a Small Planet* by Frances Moore Lappé (1971). A multi-million seller that encouraged readers to develop a diet good for the individual and the planet. It inspired Jobs to give up meat.

- *Be Here Now* by Richard Alpert (1971). A staple of the hippie movement, even inspiring a song of the same name by George Harrison. Ram Dass (as Alpert became known) expands on his theories regarding spirituality, meditation and yoga.

- *Autobiography of a Yogi* by Paramahansa Yogananda (1946). Details the Indian-born author's spiritual adventures across a life divided between spells in the East and the West. Jobs is said to have read the book – designated one of the 100 most important spiritual books of the twentieth century in a poll conducted by publishers HarperCollins – once a year after first coming across it as a teenager.

- *Cosmic Consciousness: A Study in the Evolution of the Human Mind* by Dr Richard Maurice Bucke (1901). A classic introduction to the subject of cosmic consciousness, based on the author's own mystical experience in the 1870s. He argues for the universe as a living presence rather than merely inert matter, as well as looking at the consciousness of animals and of humanity in general.

- *Meditation in Action* by Chögyam Trungpa (1969). A guide for both newcomers and experienced practitioners of Buddhist meditation by a Tibetan master. He explains how the states classically associated with meditation (clarity, discipline, energy, generosity, patience and wisdom) can equip the individual to deal with the tests of life.

- *Cutting Through Spiritual Materialism* by Chögyam Trungpa (1973). Based on a series of lectures given by Trungpa in 1970 and 1971, investigating how the conscious pursuit of spiritualism actually negates true self-knowledge.

- *The Mucusless Diet Healing System: Scientific Method of Eating Your Way to Health* by Arnold Ehret (1922). A guide that claims to show how diet impacts on health, even to the extent of curing diseases previously labelled incurable. Ehret recommends a diet of 'mucusless foods', namely fruit, herbs and starchless vegetables. It profoundly influenced Jobs' own patterns of food consumption.

- *Rational Fasting* by Arnold Ehret (1926). A further work encouraging a gradual transition to the type of diet outlined in the above title.

- *The Whole Earth Catalog*, a periodical published by Stewart Brand, principally between 1968 and 1972 (though editions did come out sporadically up to 1998). It provided information for disciples of the counterculture on where to find tools and skills. Jobs described it as 'one of the bibles of my generation' and 'sort of like Google in paperback form, thirty-five years before Google came along'. One tagline from the final edition stayed with Jobs in particular: 'Stay hungry, stay foolish.'
- *Zen Mind, Beginner's Mind* by Shunryu Suzuki (1970). A compilation of teachings by a Zen monk who ran a spiritual centre in Los Altos. Encouraging a move away from intellectualism, it is now widely considered a classic of the genre.

Meet the
Right People

'Innovation comes from people meeting up
in the hallways or calling each other at 10.30 at
night with a new idea, or because they realized
something that shoots holes in how we've
been thinking about a problem.'

STEVE JOBS

Be in the right place at the right time

When it came to pursuing his career, Jobs had the benefit of being in the right place at the right time, having grown up in California's Santa Clara Valley. By the 1970s the area had come to be known as Silicon Valley on account of the large number of tech companies that had set up business there in the preceding decades. (The name derives from the silicon transistor vital to the modern microprocessor.) Many of these businesses had strong links to Stanford, the Ivy League university situated in the vicinity. As Timothy J. Sturgeon of the Massachusetts Institute of Technology wrote in 2000: 'Perhaps the strongest thread that runs through the Valley's past and present is the drive to "play" with novel technology, which, when bolstered by an advanced engineering degree and channelled by astute management, has done much to create the industrial powerhouse we see in the Valley today.'

If Steve Jobs had not happened to be there already,

it seems likely that he would have found his way to Silicon Valley of his own accord. That said, while being in the Valley at that particular moment in history was certainly serendipitous for Jobs, it was still beholden upon him to take advantage of the situation. Simply being in the Valley was no more a guarantee of success in the technology arena than being in Hollywood is a guarantee of an Oscar.

Find friends on the same wavelength

Crucially, from a young age Jobs attracted likeminded individuals who would help him develop his interests, skills and ideas. At high school he became great friends with Bill Fernandez, the two of them wiling away hours talking over the big questions of life and undertaking science projects together. Fernandez would go on to join Apple in its very early days but will be most notable to future historians as the person who introduced Jobs and Steve Wozniak.

Wozniak, a bona fide technology geek, was in the early 1970s dreaming up plans for his own computer: reading manuals, making drawings, building circuit boards. Like Jobs, he learned by doing and didn't mind making some mistakes along the way. The two, though very different in certain fundamental respects, were – it now goes without saying – a great fit, each inspiring the other to new heights. But more of that later.

At university Jobs made still more friends who would come to play a role in the Apple story, most notably Daniel Kottke. The two not only buddied up during Jobs' brief stint at Reed but also shared the experience of that character-defining trip around India. Kottke, like Fernandez, would become one of the earliest employees of Apple a few years later.

Ask questions

Another important early influence on Jobs was an employee of Hewlett-Packard, a long-established technology giant in the Valley. One of the company's engineers, Larry Lang, lived a few doors up the road from young Steve and he took the lad under his wing, acting as an early mentor and nurturing his love of all things technical.

Among other things, Lang introduced Jobs to the wonders of Heathkits, self-assembly technology kits that had been produced by the Heath Company of Michigan since 1947. For enthusiasts intent on building their own TV receiver or clock radio or even hobbyist computer, the kits demystified the world of resistors, capacitors, vacuum tubes and transformers. For an enquiring young mind they represented a veritable cornucopia of possibilities. When Jobs was a little older, Lang also introduced him into the Hewlett-Packard Explorers' Club, which met weekly to hear talks by engineers. It was at one of these events that the twelve-year-old Jobs first set eyes on a prototype home computer.

And if the right people didn't naturally gravitate towards him, Jobs was confident enough to go out and find them for himself. While he was certainly not everyone's cup of tea – at school, perhaps to mask a lack of confidence, the quiet and introspective boy with a taste for poetry and microchips could sometimes appear arrogant and overbearing – he developed a bravado that often gave him the edge, providing him with an air of self-assuredness just when it was most needed.

This is neatly illustrated by an association he forged in his youth. After attending a Hewlett-Packard Explorers' Club gathering, Jobs set himself the task of building a frequency counter but found he was short of several vital HP parts. Deciding to strike right to the very heart of his problem, he tracked down the personal details of Bill Hewlett, founder of Hewlett-Packard, and called the Silicon Valley icon on his home number. While other unsolicited callers might have expected to receive short shrift for their cheek, Jobs shared a twenty-minute conversation with Hewlett. By the end of it he had not only secured a guarantee that he would receive all the requested parts for his frequency counter but had also won the offer of a summer job – an opportunity for which others would have killed.

Network

Jobs' ability to spot and build bonds with people who could be useful to him and his willingness to network were skills that came naturally to him, even from a young age. His instinct that the path to greatness could not be navigated alone was one that would stay with him throughout his career. For Jobs, amazing work was (with the very rarest of exceptions) done by teams of talented people sharing a vision and working in a conducive environment.

'Technology is nothing. What's important is that you have a faith in people, that they're basically good and smart, and if you give them tools, they'll do wonderful things with them.'

STEVE JOBS

While Jobs stands in his own right as one of the great technological and commercial figures of our age, there are few who would disagree that he might never have got going were it not for the different strain of genius that belonged to Steve Wozniak. Fortune surely had a hand in bringing them together, marrying the slightly older Woz's technical brilliance to Jobs' remarkable energy, ambition and instinct for what the public wanted. They stand out as one of the great double acts of industrial history, so it is worth devoting a page or two to look at the career of Woz in isolation.

Stephen Wozniak was born on 11 August 1950 in San Jose, California, growing up, like Jobs, in Santa Clara Valley. His father worked for the Lockheed Corporation – perhaps the greatest name in the US aeronautics industry at the time and deeply involved in some of the most cutting-edge and top-secret technological projects of the Cold War age – so it was hardly a surprise that the young Woz developed a fascination with all things electronic.

Like Jobs, he was intelligent and displayed potential but was easily bored by school and devoted long hours to making devices such as calculators and radios. In 1968 he enrolled at the University of Colorado but left after only a year owing to a chronic shortage of funds. He spent a further year at DeAnza Community College in Cupertino, before taking a year out to earn the money to fund a further year of study at the University of California, Berkeley. He again dropped out, however, and moved back to Silicon Valley to take up a position with Hewlett-Packard.

By then his path had started to cross with Jobs. Initially introduced by their mutual friend, Bill Fernandez, the two cemented their friendship when Jobs took Bill Hewlett's offer of a vacation job, as well as at sessions of the Homebrew Computer Club, a group of computer enthusiasts who started to meet formally in 1975, usually in the garage of one agreeable member or another.

For Woz, 1975 was something of an *annus mirabilis*. This was in no small part a result of the arrival of the MITS Altair 8800, a microcomputer to be built from kit. Its release is now widely regarded as one of the sparks that lit the personal computer revolution. Alas for Woz at the time, a basic kit cost $439, with that figure rising by several hundred dollars once you had purchased all the other bits of essential equipment. But its effect was to galvanize him to focus his attentions on creating a computer of his own. The result was Apple I, the machine that birthed Apple Computer, Inc.

By his own admission, Woz dreamed of being a great computer engineer rather than a business leader. He lacked the boundary-less ambition that drove Jobs and enjoyed using some of his newfound wealth to explore other personal interests. Fatefully for the Lockheed engineer's son, one of these interests was flying. In February 1981 Woz crashed a small aircraft he was piloting shortly after taking off from Sky Park Airport in California's Scotts Valley. He and his three passengers suffered injuries which, though not life-threatening, proved, for Woz at least, quite life-changing. These included significant temporary memory problems.

It was 1983 before Woz came back to work at Apple full-time, though he had tried his hand as a technology festival organizer in the meantime. In 1985 he and Jobs had their spectacular contribution to the IT revolution recognized when the National Technology

Award was bestowed upon them by President Ronald Reagan. A year later Woz belatedly earned his bachelor's degree in computer science and electrical engineering from the University of California, Berkeley – by which point, it would be safe to assume, he could have taught his professors more than they were able to teach him. As evidence of his unwillingness to wallow in the spotlight, he chose to go under the name of Rocky Clark during his studies, Rocky being his dog's name and Clark his then wife's maiden name.

By 1987 Woz was ready for a change and ended full-time employment with the company that had earned him unimaginable wealth and significant fame (even if it was Jobs who had firmly established himself as the 'face' of the company). Nonetheless, Wozniak remains to this day a listed company employee, picking up a relatively modest – in multi-millionaire terms, at least – annual stipend.

He threw himself into a raft of new projects in the years that followed. He worked, for instance, on a programmable remote control that he hoped would revolutionize the market, developed applications that took advantage of the fast-developing field of GPS technology, and has also been involved in telecommunications and data storage enterprises. He was, in addition, a co-founder of the Electronic Frontier Foundation, whose activities are centred on promoting technologies it believes uphold personal freedom and defending the users of such technologies if they are subject to what the organization considers unfair or baseless criminal prosecution.

Woz, who has been married four times and is the father of three children, never wanted to be in the limelight, as Jobs desired, and certainly disliked much of the baggage that went with being one of the great innovators of his time. Nonetheless, he was at the eye of a veritable technological revolution and few get such a chance to leave their imprint on history. The title of his 2006 biography perhaps says it best of all: *iWoz: From Computer Geek to Cult Icon: How I Invented the Personal Computer, Co-Founded Apple, and Had Fun Doing It.*

Mine Your Life Experience

'We used to dream about this stuff. Now we
get to build it. It's pretty great.'

STEVE JOBS

Whatever his faults, Jobs could never be accused of being backward in coming forward. He was a man who threw himself into life, putting himself in the way of experiences that he could then mine for his work. He spoke often of the importance of exposing yourself to the best things that humans have done so you can bring that experience into whatever it is you do. Indeed, he argued that the team responsible for the Mac were not tunnel-visioned über-geeks; instead, they were a gang of exceptionally broad characters – musicians, poets, artists, zoologists and historians – who, it just so happened, were also the best computer scientists in the world.

As for the über-geeks, of which there is no shortage in Silicon Valley, Jobs was vocal in his criticism of their lack of experience. Part of his life's philosophy was based around the idea that experiences are like dots that we connect to navigate our path through life. If you don't have enough dots, he believed, you end up with a pretty straight line. And Jobs was not interested in a straight-line approach to anything. For him, going on an interesting journey was key to finding your way to the best endpoint. When it came to who he wanted working with him at Apple, he looked for people with broad life experience that they could translate into a better understanding of people. He considered this crucial for devising solutions to the problems – technological or not – that real people face.

His faith in the value of personal experience informed his own life deeply. As a tenth-grader with his eye on a future in Silicon Valley, Jobs got himself part-time work in an electronics parts store. Not only did it give him an income stream but it also exposed him to the nuts and bolts of the business he had set his heart on. Beyond that, it gave him a solid grounding in the rudimentaries of business, and the importance of the bottom line. Before long he was buying electronics parts himself from a third-party supplier and selling them on to his own boss at a small profit, before helping his boss move them on to their customer base at still greater profit.

The period after he dropped out of Reed could easily have become one of lost opportunities, but not for Jobs. He mined his time there in most unexpected ways. Although he had formally left his course, he continued to attend several classes that piqued his interest. One of these was a calligraphy class. At the time, Jobs had been struck by the fact that some posters around college were far more eye-catching than others, and he became interested in the power of different fonts. When he took the calligraphy class, he did not have much of an eye on how it might inform his future but he would take the knowledge he picked up there and use it to brilliant effect years later in the design of the Apple Mac's software. The Mac would open up a galaxy of fonts to people who probably never knew such things could ever be of interest to them. The era of desktop publishing that the Mac helped usher in owed no little debt to that dot of calligraphy experience that Jobs picked up in a classroom in Oregon in the early 1970s.

Be a
Survivor

'Your time is limited, so don't waste it living someone else's life. Don't let the noise of others' opinions drown out your own inner voice.'

STEVE JOBS

Life did not always go smoothly for Steve Jobs, from his uneasy passage into the world to dropping out of college and being cast out of the company he built from nothing – not to mention the ill health that plagued his final years. Throughout it all, he proved himself to have the mentality of a survivor. He was eternally adaptable, emerging from every low to make his way towards a new high.

Always have a plan

When he dropped out at Reed after just one semester, Jobs was a young man without a plan. Yet he came to regard it as one of the pivotal moments in his life because it forced him to find a way to get by. Staying in Oregon, he slept on friends' floors until he had exhausted their hospitality and recycled soda bottles as a means of earning a few cents. To keep his head above water, he also got a fairly unglamorous job looking after equipment used in experiments by the college's psychology department. But he found selling 'blue boxes' to be a far more lucrative trade.

Jobs had started in the 'blue box' business a year earlier, in 1971. It was a joint enterprise with Woz and earned the two of them a healthy amount. There was just one drawback: what they were doing was illegal. 'Blue boxes' were developed by hackers to allow people to hijack telephone lines and make free phone calls. Woz and Jobs had read about it in a magazine and, ever ingenious, set about building their own version. As a prank, they even used the system to call the office of the Pope and almost made it through to the man himself by pretending they were Henry Kissinger.

After some tweaking and careful sourcing of parts, the dastardly duo were able to produce a box for $40 and sell it for $300. With such profit margins on offer, it was little wonder Jobs was tempted back into the business. Another unforeseen result of this shady episode was that Jobs and Woz were for many years the acceptable faces of Silicon Valley to some hackers. It has been speculated that the ties they built at this time with the likes of John Draper – who went by the sobriquet 'Captain Crunch' and was considered the brains behind the 'blue box' – kept Apple off many hackers' hit lists for a long time.

While this nefarious behaviour cannot be condoned, it does show Jobs' determination to make the best of a bad situation and his willingness to graft. Having managed to find a way to stay around the college despite no longer being part of its official student body, he made good use of his time there. He had caught the eye of the Dean, who was impressed by Jobs' evident curiosity and intellectual sparkiness, and was permitted to attend a few classes – such as the calligraphy course – as an interested onlooker.

Stick to your guns

Jobs displayed similar tenaciousness to get one of his earliest jobs back in Silicon Valley. Atari was a youthful company producing arcade games such as the tennis-based 'Pong' and Jobs wanted to work there to build up his kitty for his proposed trip to India. Fuelled by this determination, he turned up at the Atari offices and simply refused to leave until they had given him a post – a particular achievement given that Jobs did not present himself as a sharp-suited global CEO-in-the-making, but was instead in the midst of his unkempt and malodorous phase! In the end, he even managed to get Atari to contribute to his Indian travel costs: the company paid for his flight to Germany on condition that he make a brief stop-off there to troubleshoot some problems at its satellite office.

'He was a great man with incredible achievements and amazing brilliance. He always seemed to be able to say in very few words what you actually should have been thinking before you thought it.'

LARRY PAGE

Keep Your Powder Dry

'Innovation distinguishes between a leader and a follower.'

STEVE JOBS

Share what you need to …

When Jobs prepared his offensive banner for an unwitting graduation class at his high school, he no doubt envisaged a stunt of high impact. In fact, the joke fell flat when the banner was prematurely unfurled by an acquaintance who had heard Jobs boasting of the escapade. The episode taught him an important lesson: keep things on the down-low until you're ready to make your entrance.

This was a message he was keen to get through to Woz in the early days of their friendship. Leaps and bounds in the development of powerful new microprocessors had raised the possibility that the likes of Woz might construct a true personal computer all of their own – a dream that only intensified after the appearance of the Altair 8800. Woz was keen to share each stage of his progress with the members of the Homebrew Computer

Club, that band of (mostly) brothers whose motto was 'Give help to others'.

Over time, Woz found a way to hook up his machine to a monitor and keyboard, an arrangement with all the hallmarks of a modern personal computer. The urge to impress his buddies must have been all but irresistible. But Jobs stepped in to convince him to keep a little something back. He came up with a compromise: why didn't Woz sell some printed circuit boards to the Homebrew crew and let them build their own fully fledged machines themselves? This was, in effect, the seed from which the Apple computer company would grow. Had Jobs not made his plea, Woz might have given away their competitive advantage for free.

… but keep your secrets safe

Jobs remained passionate about maintaining product secrecy for the rest of his career. Some have argued that he was overly obsessed. In 2010 there was an unsavoury chain of events that began with the theft from a bar of a prototype of the upcoming iPhone 4. The prototype found its way into the hands of a journalist, Jason Chen, editor of technology blog Gizmodo, provoking extreme ire from Jobs. Chen's apartment was subsequently raided by the police, who smashed in his front door. Critics suggested that the response was excessively heavy-handed and that Jobs should have been more concerned with how the gizmo came to be lost rather than worrying that journalists were doing what comes naturally to them. But Jobs would not back down, telling AllThingsD.com:

> When this whole thing with Gizmodo happened, I got a lot of advice from people that said, 'You've got to just let it slide. You shouldn't go after a journalist because they bought stolen property and they tried to extort you.' And I thought deeply about this, and I ended up concluding that the worst thing that could possibly happen as we get big and we get a little bit more influence in the world is if we change our core values, and start 'letting it slide'. I can't do that. I'd rather quit.

For all his understandable indignation at the theft and his annoyance at Gizmodo's refusal to hand the prototype back, the underlying message was clear: Jobs valued secrecy and would chase you down if you deigned to disregard it.

The iPhone 4 debacle also underlined Jobs' frequently strained relations with journalists. It was certainly not the first time that a member of the Fourth Estate had accused him of bullying tactics. He was notoriously protective of his image and was often reluctant to grant interviews unless they coincided with product launches and came with a guarantee of coverage for the latest goody he was bringing to market.

Once upon a time, Jobs had his thunder stolen by an interloper who unfurled his handiwork before he was ready. He did everything in his power to make sure it never happened again. But he was a master at knowing just when to launch on to an unsuspecting world, so who can really blame him?

Seize
Opportunity

'We're gambling on our vision, and we would
rather do that than make "me too" products.
Let some other companies do that.'

STEVE JOBS

It goes without saying that Jobs did not lack for ambition. His first girlfriend, Chrisann Brennan, recalled how, when he was aged around seventeen, he told her that someday he would be a millionaire.

Never short on confidence or bravado, these were traits that time and again proved crucial to his success. Yet it is interesting to note that, as a young man, even Jobs could be prone to underselling himself. This is best illustrated by an anecdote dating from the time just after he had persuaded Woz to sell his bespoke circuit boards to his Homebrew Computer Club comrades. One of the Homebrewers was Paul Terrell, who ran a computer store called The Byte Shop. Jobs approached him to ask whether he would be interested in taking on a few $50 circuit boards. If they sold well, Jobs suggested, they could up the order. What he hadn't expected was for Terrell to bite his hand off. But Terrell wasn't interested in simple circuit boards; he wanted complete machines – fifty of them – and he was prepared to pay $500 for each one. An order worth $25,000 went far beyond what Jobs had thought possible.

There was a problem, too. Jobs did not know if Woz would have any chance of fulfilling the order. But the Jobs bravura kicked in and he shook on the deal there and then. Winning the business was the hard part, while fulfilling it, he was sure, could be made to happen. In this way, the legendary Apple I came to be born – a machine built for people like Woz himself, very smart geeks who could see what a thing of wonder it was. And if they weren't convinced, Jobs was on hand to persuade them.

The Jobs family home was transformed into a factory in short order. To finance this initial wave of production, Jobs sold his VW van and Woz brought in some money by selling his I IP scientific calculator. Even with this capital influx, the computer that Woz came up with lacked a number of basic features, including casing, keyboard, screen and power source. When Jobs delivered the goods to Terrell, the shop owner was anything but overwhelmed, having anticipated something with a rather more finessed look, but he stayed good to his word and paid the agreed price. The Apple adventure was underway and Jobs would rarely undersell himself again.

Jobs believed that knowing who someone's heroes were gave you a great insight into their character. We actually know quite a lot about Jobs' own icons, not least from the now legendary 'Think different' advertising campaign of the late 1990s, which featured a long list of figures who passed muster with him. The campaign featured, among others: entertainers (Bob Dylan, John Lennon and Yoko Ono, Maria Callas, Alfred Hitchcock, Jim Henson and Kermit the Frog, Louis Armstrong and Martha Graham); businessmen (Richard Branson and Ted Turner); artists (Pablo Picasso and Salvador Dalí); political leaders (Martin Luther King, Jr. and Mahatma Gandhi); architects and designers (Frank Lloyd Wright and Buckminster Fuller); a scientist (Albert Einstein); a sportsman (Muhammad Ali); and an adventuress and aviator (Amelia Earhart).

As someone with a deep understanding of the potential of technology and a rare feel for what works aesthetically, it is little surprise that Jobs also spoke of his admiration for both Michelangelo and Leonardo Da Vinci.

Michelangelo – painter of the Sistine Chapel and creator of the monumental statue of David along with heartbreaking pieces such as the *Pietà* in the Vatican – once observed: 'Every block of stone has a statue inside it and it is the task of the sculptor to discover it.' It is a sentiment that one could imagine Jobs brought to his own working life. But Jobs was impressed that, as well as mastery of the arts, Michelangelo 'knew a tremendous amount about how to cut stone at the quarry'. Da Vinci similarly straddled the arts and sciences, arguably like no human before or since, as proficient in designing prototype flying machines as he was in creating artworks including the *Mona Lisa*. Both represented for Jobs that meeting of the arts and sciences so fundamental to his own success.

Here are the profiles of four other of Jobs' heroes, all of them technology giants of the nineteenth and/or twentieth centuries whose stories not only inspired Jobs but whose lives and philosophies had distinct parallels with his own:

THOMAS EDISON
When Jobs was backpacking his way around

India he reported an epiphany that maybe Thomas Edison had actually done a lot more to improve the world than 'Karl Marx and Neem Karoli Baba [an Indian guru who came to Western prominence in the 1960s and 1970s] put together'.

Jobs has often been described as the Edison of our age. Whatever the validity of the statement, Jobs was an admirer of the great American inventor, who was honoured with an appearance in the 'Think different' campaign. It should probably come as little surprise, for the two men certainly covered common philosophical ground. 'There is always a better way,' Edison once noted, a belief that underpinned Jobs' career many decades later.

Thomas Alva Edison was born in 1847 in Ohio and, again in common with Jobs, grew up as something of an outsider. The seventh child of his parents, he was considered a troublesome if sparky pupil and was eventually expelled from school. Home-schooled by his mother, Edison showed great potential in the sciences but his progress was held back by a deteriorating hearing problem. Given a job as a telegraph operator, he saved his money and built a laboratory in which he spent much of his free time, patenting his first invention, an electric vote recorder, when he was twenty-one years old.

In 1871 Edison built a large factory and laboratory complex in Newark, New Jersey, and three years later had his first big commercial success with a new telegraph system. He sank the profits into a laboratory at Menlo Park that became known as the 'Invention Factory'. Among its output was the phonograph, an improved telephone transmitter, an electric pen and, most famously of all, the electric light bulb. Never one to stand still – a touch of the Jobs once again – in 1886 he built another laboratory complex at West Orange, New Jersey. Here his team carried out groundbreaking work in the field of motion pictures, as well as producing a storage battery that proved to be the most profitable project of his life. He even had time for a dose of failure, undertaking a misbegotten spell in the iron mining business in the 1890s.

By the time of his death in 1931, Edison had 1,093 patents to his name – putting even Jobs' extensive collection in the shade. Foreshadowing the ethos that would dominate at Apple, Edison once told an assistant who wanted guidance on the lab rules: 'Hell! There ain't no rules around here! We are tryin' to accomplish somep'n!'

HENRY FORD

Another school of thought says that if Jobs wasn't the Edison of his age, he was its Henry Ford instead. While it might not be a perfect fit, the parallels between the two men are undeniable. Ford, after all, was the man who in 1924 said: 'The most dangerous notion a young man can acquire is that there is no more room for originality. There is no large room for anything else.'

Born in Michigan in 1863, Henry Ford left school to work on the family farm when he was fifteen. However, it was not long before he took up an apprenticeship in a Detroit machine shop, fixing clocks and watches in his spare time to make some extra pocket money. After a brief and unhappy return to farming on land given to him by his father, he came back to Detroit and took a job with the Edison Illuminating Company. It was at this time that he became fascinated by the burgeoning motorcar business, and in 1896 he successfully built his own vehicle in a shed in his garden.

Commercial success remained elusive, however, and Ford is counted among America's most famous bankrupts. But in 1903 he started a new company and hit pay dirt with his Model A car. Next came the legendary Model T, which became the company's sole production model from 1909 onwards. By tweaking his methods of mass production, it became the cheapest car on the market.

By the mid-1920s the Ford Motor Company was rolling out 10,000 cars each day, some three-fifths of the entire US output. In 1927, the fifteen-millionth Model T was sold. But a reluctance to develop new models – most un-Jobs-like – ensured that the competition was soon breathing down Ford's neck. He died in 1948.

In relation to market research, Jobs liked to cite one of Ford's most famous lines: 'If I had asked my customers what they wanted, they would have said a faster horse.'

EDWIN LAND

Though perhaps a lesser global figure than the two giants above, Edwin Land was a bona fide hero to Jobs, who admired the way he built up his company, Polaroid, from nothing and kept it at the top of the tree for decades.

Land was born in Bridgeport, Connecticut, in 1909. In 1932 he and one of his university tutors set up the Land Wheelwright Laboratories to capitalize on his work with light filters. In 1937 the company was rebranded as the Polaroid Corporation. It was Land's ambition that it 'stand at the intersection of art and science'. Like Jobs, he believed that business should be a partnership between dreamers and managers, with the latter creating the working environment in which the former could prosper.

After spending a year at Harvard studying chemistry, Land dropped out and headed for New York to make his fortune. There he invented inexpensive light filters that brought the era of instant photography a good deal closer. He briefly returned to Harvard but lacked motivation for the academic life and left without receiving his degree. (Though, as a sign of the high regard in which the scientific community held him, he was known as Dr Land throughout his career.) His Polaroid instant camera hit the shops in 1948 and the company remained at the forefront of photographic developments under his guidance until he was manoeuvred into resigning in 1980, following the failure of an instant movie system. He died in 1991.

According to a *Forbes* article of 1987, Land's distinctly Jobsian motto was: 'Don't do anything that someone else can do. Don't undertake a project unless it is manifestly important and nearly impossible.'

AKIO MORITA

Akio Morita was the founder of Sony and led the electronics company to a position of global domination. He and Jobs were friends – Morita personally gave Jobs one of the original Walkmans – and as John Sculley, one-time Apple CEO, would later say: '… he had really the same kind of high-end standards that Steve did and respect for beautiful products.' Of Jobs, Sculley noted: 'He didn't want to be IBM. He didn't want to be Microsoft. He wanted to be Sony.'

Morita was born in Nagoya in 1921 and seemed destined to work in his family's three-centuries-old sake business. He was far more interested in electronics, however, and graduated in physics from the Osaka Imperial University. During active service in the Second World War, he met Masru Ibuka, an electrical engineer who would become Woz to his Jobs. After the war, the two went into business and founded the Tokyo Telecommunications Engineering Corp.

With Morita focusing on the financial and marketing side of things business was slow to begin with, but in 1950 they enjoyed an upturn with the first magnetic tape recorder in the Japanese market. Greater success followed with the 1955 release of a pocket-sized transistor radio (just as long as you had quite big pockets). In 1958 the company changed its name to Sony and three years later it became the first Japanese company to be listed on the New York Stock Exchange.

Morita and his family moved to the US in 1963 so that he could better understand the American marketplace. Sony firmly established itself as a global leader with its TVs, video recorders and music systems but arguably the company's finest moment came in 1979 with the release of the Sony Walkman that so fascinated Jobs and went on to sell over a quarter of a billion units. At the time of Morita's death in

1999, Sony was rated America's number one consumer brand.

There are two Morita quotes in particular that have more than a hint of Jobs about them. The first relates to the role of a manager within a business: 'We will try to create conditions where persons could come together in a spirit of teamwork, and exercise to their heart's desire their technological capacity.' The second, meanwhile, concerns innovation: 'The public does not know what is possible. We do.'

Never
Stand Still

'If you haven't found it yet, keep looking. Don't settle.
As with all matters of the heart, you'll know when
you find it. And, like any great relationship, it just
gets better and better as the years roll on.'

STEVE JOBS

Play the percentages …

Now convinced they had a business and not merely a hobby, Woz and Jobs were determined to put things on a solid base. For one thing, this meant observing the legal niceties of establishing a company. But Woz was nervous in case he should be accused of using any of Hewlett-Packard's ideas in his non-HP work. So he arranged a meeting with the HP management to showcase what would become Apple I. While they were impressed with what he had achieved, they decided it wasn't a product for them and so the path opened up for Jobs and Woz to strike out on their own.

As with their previous enterprises, the two decided on a democratic split of profits straight down the middle. But then they decided to bring in a third partner to ensure that the company could not be paralyzed by any disagreement between the two of them. In came Ron Wayne, a manager whom Jobs knew from his time at Atari, his head turned by the offer of a 10 per cent stake. The documentation signed, Apple Computer, Inc. came into being on 1 April 1976 – April Fools' Day. But there was perhaps only one fool that day: Wayne, who got cold feet and sold his stake in the company for about $2,500.

… but keep things moving

Jobs and Woz recognized the importance of momentum and both kept up an extraordinary early pace. The Apple I complete, Woz was soon on to his next project: a faster, better machine with sound, improved graphics, far greater programmability and the potential for extensive 'bolting on' by users. This was to be the Apple II, which would go on to shake the world.

But Jobs and Woz were not to know just how big an impact it would make while it was still in the development phase. So keen were they to see where they stood against the opposition that they booked tickets to a major computer exhibition in Atlantic City in the summer of 1976. While exhibiting the Apple I, Jobs characteristically decreed that they should keep the Apple II out of the limelight until they were ready to roll out the finished product. Having peeked at the work of their rivals, he was convinced that Woz was creating something far ahead of anything else on the market.

Don't rest on your laurels

Meanwhile, Jobs sought to reinvest the moderate profits generated by Apple I straight back into the company. They soon moved out of the Jobs' garage, renting an office in nearby Cupertino. If Apple was not yet operating as a slick corporate operation, it was at least starting to look more like one.

Jobs and Woz also set about expanding the staff. In came old school friend Bill Fernandez, who had garnered experience over at Hewlett-Packard. Next in was Reed alumnus Daniel Kottke, to bring some order to the company's accounting processes. Jobs, meanwhile, styled himself as director of marketing with Woz as director of engineering. Outsiders were beginning to notice the start-up. In July 1976 Apple was featured in an edition of *Interface* magazine, which described it as 'a well-disciplined, financially sound group that is opening new vistas in computer hardware, software, and service to their clientele'.

There was a new mover and shaker in Silicon

Valley. Paul Terrell's order may have come out of the blue but Jobs had been sure to seize the moment. Backed by Woz's hot streak of innovation, Jobs didn't bask in the adulation or enjoy the still fairly small fruits of their labour. He understood that there was a long road ahead and that they had only just got the wheels turning; now the hard work began to get them turning faster.

'It's like the world lost a John Lennon – I mean Steve was clearly the most outstanding business thinker and almost everybody high up in the technology business recognized that somehow he had the ability to think out new ways of doing things, not just ways to improve what we have, do a better version of something, but do it in a totally different way that the world would swing towards.'

STEVE WOZNIAK

Dream Big

'Small thinkers never do big things.'

STEVE JOBS

By the time the Apple II was in development, the company needed some serious finance. To this end, Jobs and Woz were put in touch with Don Valentine, a venture capitalist who played a key role in developing Jobs' 'dream big' philosophy. Courting Valentine's investment, Jobs told him of Apple's plans to sell as many as a couple of thousand computers a year, a seemingly ambitious claim at the time seeing as the Apple I had done about a tenth of that figure. But it impressed Valentine little. He had a mantra: 'Big thinkers often do big things. Small thinkers never do big things.' Was Apple run, he wondered, by small thinkers?

In the end, he decided not to invest – probably not his best day's work – but saw the potential and put the company in contact with another professional investor, Mike Markkula, who had heritage as a marketing man for Intel. Markkula promptly guaranteed Apple a credit line of a quarter of a million dollars, on the condition that Woz devoted himself to the business full-time. But Woz was comfortable in his position at Hewlett-Packard. He earned decent money and, with a wife to support, the appeal of a regular pay cheque was strong. Was 'small thinking' going to be Apple's downfall after all?

Markkula was determined that this would not be the case. He spoke of the emergence of a once-in-a-generation industry and told them he wanted them all to ride the rollercoaster. Such talk was lapped up by a receptive Jobs, who went on a mission to gather a small army comprising mutual friends and members of the Wozniak family. Together they arm-twisted Woz into coming to work on the Apple project full-time. Woz, who knew he wanted to create rather than manage, was persuaded that Jobs and Markkula would look after the 'exec' side of things. He finally wilted under the pressure and agreed to leave behind his HP security net.

In January 1977, Markkula joined Apple alongside Jobs and Woz, each taking a third share in the business. Where Apple I sold about 200 units in total, retailing at $666.66 (a relatively short production run that ensures they are now highly prized, with one auctioned for $640,000 in 2012), within nine months of Markkula's arrival, Apple II boasted sales of over three-quarters of a million dollars. Twelve months later and sales were up to about $8 million.

The story of Apple has helped to define the story of the entire global technology sector since the 1970s. Nonetheless, the fortunes of a few companies – each of them a giant in its own right – have been more than usually intertwined with those of Steve Jobs. So let's take a moment to consider, albeit briefly, the fates of Apple and four other companies: Hewlett-Packard, IBM, Microsoft and Xerox.

Apple

From plucky outsider to global megastar, Apple is by far and away the world's most valuable technology company. As of May 2012, it was valued at $526 billion by market capitalization (according to Google Finance) and in 2011 was temporarily the largest company of any type on the planet, before losing top spot to Exxon Mobil. In 2002 Jobs told the *New York Times* what he thought was the secret of Apple's success: 'We're the only company that owns the whole widget – the hardware, the software and the operating system. We can take full responsibility for the user experience. We can do things that the other guys can't do.'

HEWLETT-PACKARD

Founded, like Apple, out of a garage, HP appeared in Palo Alto in 1939 as the baby of Bill Reddington Hewlett and Dave Packard. One of the founding institutions of Silicon Valley, the company introduced the HP 9100A in 1968, one of the world's first mass-produced computers (although it was marketed as a desktop calculator). The firm gave early job opportunities to both Woz and Jobs but infamously turned down the option to buy a stake in the Apple I. Nonetheless, HP found itself a prominent position in the PC market, producing computers, companion hardware such as printers, and original software. Merging with Compaq in 2000, it is today, by some measures, the largest personal computer manufacturer on the planet by unit sales. However, with a value by global capitalization of $44 billion in 2012 (Google Finance), it has been dwarfed by the company set up by two of its alumni.

MICROSOFT

Microsoft was launched in 1975, about a year before Apple, by Bill Gates and Paul Allen. The two tech geniuses approached Micro

Instrumentation and Telemetry Systems (MITS) claiming they could create a BASIC interpreter for the company's new Altair 8800 computer. Having made the boast, they then set about making it true. Eschewing the 'complete package' philosophy of Apple, Microsoft focused on creating software to be used with others' hardware – a market in which it remains the undisputed king. When the company sold its shares to the public in 1986 – two years after the release of Microsoft Windows – it was valued so highly that at least three employees became instant billionaires while some 12,000 became millionaires. The introduction of the Microsoft Office suite in 1990 only helped secure its market position, and from the mid-1990s the company took on the challenges and opportunities presented by the internet with gusto. For a while it seemed as if Microsoft had vanquished Apple in the commercial battle of the computer geeks, but the incredible product roster emerging from Jobs' second spell at Apple changed the landscape. Apple overtook Microsoft as the world's most valuable tech company by market capitalization in 2010 and then forged ahead so that, by 2012, it was valued at more than double the $244 billion of Microsoft (Google Finance).

IBM

International Business Machines Corporation (IBM) began operations in 1911 as the Computing Tabulating Recording Company. It is credited with an admirable array of game-changing inventions, from the automated teller machine and the floppy disk to the electronic keypunch and the Watson artificial intelligence program. IBM employees have picked up five Nobel prizes along the way. An established computing giant long before Apple was even a glint in Steve Jobs' eye – indeed, before Steve Jobs was a glint in anyone's eye – it released its first personal computer (the IBM 5150) on to the market relatively late in 1981. Backed by its trusted name, sales were impressive and the machine became a staple of offices and homes across the world. As of May 2012, IBM was given a healthy market capitalization value of $224 billion (Google Finance). However, that left it third, just behind Microsoft and a long way off Apple.

XEROX

Xerox had it all to lose in terms of the personal computer and, one might argue, that is just what it did. Founded in 1906 as the Haloid Photographic Company and known as Xerox from 1961, the company introduced the first mass-market desktop printer in 1963, with a laser printer following six years later. The groundbreaking Xerox PARC opened in 1970, developing the mouse and the graphic interface that would underpin the personal computer industry for decades.

Alas, the company put its best state-of-the-art technology into a machine, the Xerox 8010 Star, which was far too expensive for the average household, costing $16,000 when it hit the market in 1981. In the burgeoning PC arena, the company was soon eclipsed by the likes of Apple, IBM and Microsoft and, perhaps wisely, focused its attentions instead on document management (printing, photocopying, etc.), a sector in which it remains a world leader. However, as a company it is valued at about one-fiftieth the value of Apple, with a market capitalization value in 2012 of just under $10 billion.

Cultivate Your Brand

'Every once in a while a revolutionary
product comes along that changes everything …
Apple's been very fortunate in that it's
introduced a few of these.'

STEVE JOBS

From the outset, Jobs recognized the importance of building Apple's identity. For him the business was not simply about flogging products but selling ideas, ambitions, dreams. Virtually every product has a shelf life but the relationship between company and customers need not, as long as the customers believe they can expect something special and the company keeps supplying it.

Jobs was one of the modern masters of brand-building. Of course the products were central to the enterprise. If Woz had not come up with the Apples I and II, the company would have been as good as finished before it had even got started. Equally, if the company had not come up with the iMac, iPod, iPad *et al* in the years around the turn of the millennium, it would not today be the giant that it palpably is. But beyond its products, the Apple brand now exists to some extent as an entity in its own right – almost as shorthand for an approach to life.

The mere name Apple conjures up notions of sleek design, cutting-edge technology, creativity, innovation, coolness. Consider the slogan Apple used as early as 1977: 'Simplicity is the ultimate sophistication.' A quote sometimes attributed to Leonardo da Vinci, its use showed considerable confidence on the part of Apple. This was not a company looking to shift its upcoming Apple II on the back of techno-babble or boasts about the machine's design specifications. Instead, it offers an idea, an aspiration. 'We have made the complex simple', it seems to suggest, 'and you will look extremely sophisticated for owning one.' Furthermore, it is a slogan that fits the Apple ethos as much today as it did back then. By such means, the company has come to exist conceptually, in the same way that a brand such as Coca-Cola has come to encapsulate the American dream for vast swathes of the world and Rolls-Royce is synonymous with luxury. It is an achievement to which most of the rest of the tech sector can only aspire.

Jobs started strongly as a brand-builder and it was a skill that never deserted him. Product lines come and go but ideas stay around a lot longer. In 1997 he told *Time* magazine: 'Apple is about people who think "outside the box", people who want to use computers to help them change the world, to help them create things that make a difference, and not just to get a job done.'

How many other technology CEOs could have said that and been taken seriously? But Jobs was not just any other technology CEO …

Even Apple's name is not run-of-the-mill. Consider some of the other giants of computing; some take the name of their founders (Hewlett-Packard or Dell); others choose names that leave you in no doubt as to the sector in which they operate (Microsoft or IBM – an acronym for International Business Machines). Apple, though, sounds nothing like your standard high-tech company. So how did it come about?

Jobs and Woz were scrabbling around for a suitable moniker ahead of the release of what became Apple I in 1976. It was selected while Wozniak was giving Jobs a lift in his car one day. A few ideas were being thrown around, mostly with a more traditional computer-y ring to them. Had things worked out differently, we may have had the Matrix Electronics iPod or the Executek iPad. But the two company founders decided none of these alternatives was quite up to the task.

Jobs, meanwhile, was deep into his fruitarian lifestyle and was just returning from one of his occasional stays at the All One Farm, his old college friend Robert Friedland's apple farm a little way from Portland. No doubt with apples firmly at the forefront of his mind, Jobs threw it in as a suggestion. It was, he argued, fun and unintimidating, and suggestive of spirit. Others have subsequently pointed out that it also got them into the phonebook ahead of Jobs' former employee, Atari!

Wozniak immediately put up a warning flag: what of the Beatles' Apple company? But try as they might to alight on something better, nothing seemed to fit quite as well. It was, in many ways, a stroke of genius. At one level, the apple is a symbol of nature, purity, goodness. In Biblical terms, it is, at least in the popular imagination, the fruit of knowledge. Then there is the association with intellectual pursuits, not least Sir Isaac Newton's discovery of gravity. Indeed, the original Apple logo was an ornate depiction of Newton sitting beneath an apple tree waiting for inspiration to strike. The company ultimately decided to settle on an image of an apple with a bite taken out of it, a fun pictorial play on the 'byte' of computer memory.

Besides its multi-layered meanings, the adoption of the Apple name set the company apart from its rivals from the beginning.

This was a business that approached things in a different way, a business that was ... not Executek. However, as it turned out, Woz's concerns about conflict with the Beatles were well placed, for the surviving members of the great band would go on to sue the company. As a result, in 1981 Apple Computer agreed to keep out of the music business.

But by the end of that decade, issues over the use of Apple machines in music production saw a new legal spat that cost Apple Computer over $25 million in legal settlement. When the iTunes store opened in 2003, another battle became inevitable but was finally resolved in 2007 with an agreement on use of trademarks. It was not until 2010, however, that the Beatles' music at last became available on iTunes. For a conflict that ran for years, cost millions and caused a lot of anguish, it is difficult to believe that either Apple did much damage to the other's business outside of the courtroom.

Stay at the Top

Build
Beautiful

'Your work is going to fill a large part of your life, and the only way to be truly satisfied is to do what you believe is great work. And the only way to do great work is to love what you do.'

STEVE JOBS

Take pride

When it came to keeping standards high, Jobs was relentless and, on occasion, obsessive. If you were a carpenter, he liked to argue, and you built yourself a beautiful chest of drawers, would you back it with a piece of plywood or would you use the same quality of wood as on the front and sides? To a real craftsman, it does not matter that no one is ever going to see the back of the chest of drawers. The carpenter knows what is there and that is enough of an incentive to carry on using the best quality wood he can. Such were the standards that Jobs demanded of himself and all of those with whom he worked.

When the Apple II was in the production stage, for instance, he rejected circuit boards that he considered not easy enough on the eye – even though he knew the machines' purchasers would never see them. When the Apple II was perfected to his satisfaction, he made sure all the engineers who had worked on it signed the machine's innards, just as great artists historically signed their work.

Demand perfection

Though it was Woz who, to all intents and purposes, oversaw the creation of the Apples I and II, Jobs was far more hands-on in the creation of the Macintosh. At the time, most of Apple's energies were being expended on the Lisa project – which supposedly stood for 'Local Integrated Systems Architecture' but which was, of course, a tribute to the daughter for whom Jobs was struggling to be a good dad – a machine that would ultimately fail to set the world alight. In Jobs' mind, the reason why the Mac emerged from the shadows and made such an impact was simple: 'The Lisa people wanted to do something great. The Mac people wanted to do something insanely great. The difference shows.'

Jobs always had high ambitions for the Mac, which became the first mass-market machine to use a mouse to navigate a graphic interface. In his search for perfection, he made demands on his team that would strain the resilience of even the most dedicated. He drove Chris Espinosa, one of the company's hotshot programmers, to distraction with his continual tweaking of the Mac's calculator application. In the end Espinosa created a program that he wryly called 'The Steve Jobs Roll-Your-Own-Calculator Construction Set', which allowed his boss to play with the minutiae of the interface. At last Jobs came up with something he was happy with and life went on. But for anyone who doubted the wisdom of putting so much effort into such a seemingly minor function, the calculator became the Apple standard on its machines for a great many years to come. Here was the back of the carpenter's chest of drawers.

This streak of perfectionism was just as evident on Jobs' return to the company after his hiatus. He would tell of how his engineers on the iMac project responded to its early designs by coming up with a dozen or more reasons why it couldn't work and what would need to be redesigned. Jobs, though, knew in his heart that it could work and characteristically demanded that it be made to do so. Compromise was a dirty word to him.

Love what you do

Jobs realized that maintaining passion for your work was a prerequisite for success. He spoke of how doing something great is a time-consuming and difficult undertaking. If the passion, the love for what you're doing, goes, then you simply give up. He also understood that maintaining such passion goes hand in hand with having fun. When Jobs got his early break with Atari after dropping out of Reed College, he was responding to an advert that included the phrase 'have fun and make money'. It was a sentiment guaranteed to appeal to him and one he took with him into management. Jobs could be a tough taskmaster and sometimes an abrasive character, but he got the best out of people by giving them the space to enjoy themselves creatively.

Stay focused

Throughout Apple's – and his own – meteoric rise, Jobs remained at all times a realist. He was devoted to pushing back the boundaries of what is possible but had no time for pursuing the impossible. Pragmatism was never to become a hostage of the search for perfection.

This was amply demonstrated during the development phase of the Mac project. As we have seen, Jobs went to enormous lengths to make sure it was all that it could be but the project soon slipped unacceptably from its schedule. One of the most serious implications of this was that, in accordance with an agreement between the two companies, Microsoft might be able to introduce its own graphic interface first and so steal much of the Mac's thunder. This was clearly unacceptable so Jobs cajoled his team into speeding up their work and getting the machine out on time. With deadlines to be met, he extolled them: 'Real artists ship.' Meaning: there is little point in spending time innovating if you can't deliver the goods.

'I think we're having fun. I think our customers really like our products. And we're always trying to do better.'

STEVE JOBS

Look Around
for Inspiration

'Why aren't you doing anything with this?'

STEVE JOBS

Jobs was an innovator and an inspirer of innovation. But he was also an improver of what was already there. That is to say, he was quite happy to borrow the ideas of others and make them his own. It is in this light that we should consider his fondness for a quote from perhaps the greatest twentieth-century artist, Pablo Picasso: 'Good artists copy. Great artists steal.'

Jobs surely had these words ringing in his mind one day towards the end of 1979 when he undertook a trip that has come to form part of the folklore of Apple. On that particular day, Jobs and a colleague by the name of Bill Atkinson rolled up at Xerox PARC – the research arm of the technology giant Xerox – for a tour of the facility. At the end of the visit, so the story goes, Jobs went home with a head full of new ideas that he developed into the Apple Macintosh. Xerox missed the boat and Apple became the company that we know today.

It is a great story, no doubt. But surely too good

to be true? Well, yes – but only just. By 1979, Apple was hot stuff in Silicon Valley and Jobs had agreed to Xerox buying a million dollars worth of shares – but the terms and conditions of the deal demanded the promise of a tour of Xerox PARC on Coyote Hill Road in Palo Alto. This included a presentation of Xerox's groundbreaking Xerox Alto personal computer, demonstrated by an engineer called Larry Tesler.

What Jobs and Atkinson saw amazed them. While computers of the day relied on a keyboard with which users typed commands, here was a machine that instead employed a system of on-screen icons that could be selected using a thing called a mouse. These icons then opened up windows filled with menus from which the user could choose a command.

Xerox knew they were on to something but weren't exactly sure what it was. Eventually the Alto went on general sale in 1981 but it was slow and cumbersome and ultimately flopped, Xerox soon leaving the personal computer market altogether. But the boys from Apple realized they had seen the future. 'Why aren't you doing anything with this?' Jobs had asked Tesler during his visit. 'This is the greatest thing. This is revolutionary.'

So Jobs set about getting together a team that could create a mouse that was easier to manipulate, more durable and cheaper than the one at Xerox PARC. The company also set to work on refining a digital interface to change computing forever. The result, five years later, was the Macintosh – and the rest, as they say, is history. For the record, Tesler was so frustrated by what he perceived as a lack of vision at Xerox and so impressed by what Jobs had to say that he joined the Apple staff.

Jobs was also highly adept at gaining inspiration from companies with seemingly little overlap with Apple. For instance, he once spent a fruitful day perusing the household gadgets and gizmos on sale in Macy's department store, which helped inspire the decision to case the Apple II in plastic rather than the metal that was customary for IT casing at the time. Later on, the groundbreaking candy-coloured casings of the iMac would owe more than a little to an Apple staff visit to a jelly bean factory.

'Again and again over the last four decades, Steve Jobs saw the future and brought it to life long before most people could even see the horizon.'

MICHAEL BLOOMBERG

Before Jobs got to the stage of interviewing potential employees, candidates had already undergone a vigorous selection process. Applicants needed to demonstrate exceptional personal and professional qualities, with first-rate recommendations also highly valued.

Having made it to interview, candidates could expect a thorough grilling, all done with typical Jobs idiosyncrasy. He used the process to test just how quickly candidates could think on their feet. A classic Apple interview question, for instance, was: 'How might you go about investigating a technology without giving away to anyone that you are investigating it?' Such puzzlers soon separated the wheat from the chaff.

Jobs would also expect an encyclopaedic knowledge of Apple, its products and its ethos. He delved into the interviewees' personalities, too, asking open-ended questions such as: 'Why are you here?' On occasion he could be remarkably cruel. In one infamous interview during his initial spell at Apple, he barracked a candidate he had not taken to, interrupting the interviewee's answers by murmuring:

'Gobble, gobble, gobble'. Furthermore – and presumably in contravention of significant chunks of employment law – Jobs demanded to know when the interviewee had lost his virginity, if in fact he was still a virgin, and whether he had ever taken LSD.

At the end of the interview process, Jobs carefully considered all the data he had accumulated on the candidate but made his final decision based on gut instinct. Of course, few interviewees got to a one-to-one with the boss without the requisite technical abilities – but would they actually fit into the Apple organization? Would they put the company first? These were the key questions, and only a select band made the grade.

Build a
Winning Team

'I found that there were these incredibly great people at doing certain things, and that you couldn't replace one of these people with fifty average people.'

STEVE JOBS

Steve Jobs understood a basic truth: Apple could never be more than the sum of its people and their ideas. Regardless of the extent of his personal drive and his not inconsiderable skills, the greatness he hungered for could only be achieved by a team – and an extraordinarily talented team at that. Jobs believed that his key management duty was to assemble a winning team and then create an environment in which each individual would feel he or she was undertaking important work, with equally talented people, and as part of an overall vision.

He was convinced that the best people can achieve exponentially more than the merely competent or capable, and so invested much energy in seeking them out. He considered recruitment to be among the most challenging demands of his role and rarely permitted himself to delegate it to others. For a man with an undoubted touch of the 'control freak' about him, Jobs did not trust anyone as much as himself to sniff out the true *crème de la crème* of candidates. And a person's talent had to be combined with a willingness to be stretched: not for Jobs a shrinking violet happy to sit quietly for five or ten years awaiting their opportunity. Instead, in his own words, he wanted an individual who would thrive in a situation where he was in 'a little over his head'.

Jobs' resolution to have the best team around him was acutely evident after he had wrestled control of the Macintosh project from its previous leader, Jef Raskin – the man who had given the project its name, inspired by '[his] favorite kind of eatin' apple, the succulent McIntosh'. Jobs was determined to triumph with what was something of a secondary project within Apple at the time – behind the Lisa project – and the first step to securing this was to handpick a creative team, even if it came at the expense of what were now rival Apple operations. For instance, he decided he wanted Andy Hertzfeld, who was working on the Apple II. Having interviewed him in the morning, Jobs offered Hertzfeld a job in the afternoon. Hertzfeld eagerly accepted, explaining that he could join the project after tying up a few loose ends in his current post. Jobs responded by pulling the power cord from Hertzfeld's Apple II, losing all of his unsaved work, and directed him to his new desk. The message was clear: Hertzfeld was now on Jobs' squad and was not to be distracted by anything else.

But Jobs' recruitment record was by no means perfect. After Mike 'Scotty' Scott, Apple president since 1977, quit the company in 1981, Jobs undertook a long search for the right person to replace him. His head was turned by the great strides that Pepsi-Cola was then making against its great rival, Coca-Cola. So he approached Pepsi's main man, John Sculley, wooing him over a period of several months. With Sculley wavering as to his next move, Jobs laid down a poser for him: would he rather spend a life selling fizzy pop or would he like to make a dent in the universe?

Sculley signed a highly lucrative contract and joined Apple in 1983. By 1985, however, the firm needed a hit following the relatively unsuccessful commercial performances of the Apple III and Lisa models; amid that pressure, Jobs and Sculley were not getting along. Indeed, Sculley would report to the board that Jobs was behaving like 'a petulant brat'. Jobs, deciding against seizing the moral high ground, retaliated by calling him a 'bozo'. It was a rare instance when Jobs apparently met his match. He was removed from the Mac project and essentially cut adrift from the company he loved. All the while, Apple's stock was falling and Sculley was looking less and less like the man to save the day. Jobs, no doubt, wished he'd left him selling fizzy pop.

Of course, Apple's relative wilderness years in the 1990s ensured that Jobs' finest bit of recruitment was still to come – recruiting himself back into the company in 1997. Once back in situ, he set about a comprehensive overhaul of the board and the installation of 'his people'. Personnel would be as critical to Jobs' Apple 2.0 project as they had been in the company's first incarnation.

For a man who so understood the value of people to a business, Jobs nonetheless developed quite a reputation for being prickly, difficult and frequently unreasonable. In looking at how he dealt with people – both on a professional and a personal basis – his behaviour is sometimes best considered in terms of a 'how not to' guide.

A man of undoubted passion and sometimes short temper, Jobs would no doubt have conceded himself that his 'people management' skills fell short of what they should be at certain times and with particular individuals. All that said, he commanded enormous respect and trust among the vast majority who worked alongside and underneath him. He was able to instil in people the sense that they were on a collective mission, a joint quest for perfection, and thus many of his excesses were overlooked. Jobs spoke of how his role was not to be easy on people but to make them better. It is against this aim that his management style is best judged.

Don't lose your cool

One of the dark sides of Steve Jobs was that he could be volatile and unkind. He was not above humiliating people in front of their colleagues and was repeatedly accused of usurping others' ideas for his own glorification. He hugely upset Jef Raskin, the man originally in charge of the Macintosh project, who sent a memo to Apple president Mike Scott stating that Jobs' performance as a manager was 'dreadful' and accusing him of attacking those whose ideas he didn't understand while claiming credit for the ideas of others. (As we have also seen, Jobs proved to have more muscle in the resulting arm wrestle and Raskin quickly moved on. This in itself no doubt represents a valuable lesson of sorts: if you're going to upset people, make sure your position is strong enough to withstand any retaliation. On this occasion Jobs won; on other occasions he didn't.)

Don't lose perspective

Jobs could also be coldly ruthless. When he oversaw a restructuring of Pixar in the early 1990s, he notoriously sacked over 40 per cent of the company without notice or severance pay. Redundancy is never much fun, but he did little to make it any easier for all those people who had to go home and tell their families that they didn't have a job anymore. He could also be monstrously petty, as when he threw his toys out of the pram after Mike Scott introduced a payroll system to tighten up payment processes in the early days of Apple. It happened that Woz was designated employee no. 1, while Jobs was no. 2. This really was small stuff that should not have been sweated but an enraged Jobs took the issue up with Scott, who, to his credit, refused to back down.

Don't lose your audience

Those who worked with Jobs on the Macintosh project were exposed to a good many of his character frailties. Many complained of his changeability: what was a terrible idea one day could become a stroke of genius the next – and quite possibly Jobs' stroke of genius rather than anyone else's. But the Mac project also exemplifies many of his skills as a manager. The end product was so great that it could be said to have justified the means. Indeed Bud Tribble, part of the team behind the Mac, spoke of how brilliant Jobs was at persuading the gang that they were on the brink of creating something great. 'He can convince anyone of practically anything,' Tribble recalled, before wryly noting: 'It wears off when he's not around.' It was this ability to inspire people to new heights that was perhaps Jobs' greatest strength.

It is clear Steve Jobs was not a man who went into business to make friends. But he was someone who valued people, which makes his sporadic people-management failings all the harder to understand. As Richard Branson commented to *ShortList* in 2012: 'Too many business leaders are too quick to jump down people's throats, or rule by fear, which is foolish.' He added: 'Steve Jobs was quite ruthless, and did very well despite that, but that isn't the way it should be done.'

But did Steve Jobs achieve his goal of creating the climate in which people do better things than they thought they were capable of? Undoubtedly so.

Master the Money (So it Doesn't Master You)

'Being the richest man in the cemetery doesn't matter to me … Going to bed at night saying we've done something wonderful … that's what matters to me.'

STEVE JOBS

Don't do it for the money alone

The quote above, taken from an interview with the *Wall Street Journal* in 1999, is, it might be argued, an easy sentiment to hold when your bank balance looks like a telephone number. But save for the odd personal jet and luxury yacht, it is widely acknowledged that Steve Jobs lived a fairly humble existence when compared to some of his peers. He lived, for instance, in a house that was more ordinary than palatial and dressed no more grandly than the average person who bought his products.

His ambivalent relationship with money was a theme he came back to time and again. In 1996 he spoke of how he had made his first million by twenty-three and his first hundred million by twenty-five, but that this was not important because he never did it for the money. And in the 2000s he observed: 'I'm the only person I know that's lost a quarter of a billion dollars in one year … It's very character-building.'

Jobs also spoke of his dislike of the notion of entrepreneurs – a word he associated with opportunists looking to start a company with the overriding goal of selling it on or going public for personal gain. It would be hard to argue that a quick buck was ever his overriding motivation. But let's not take his word for it. Consider the judgement of Walt Mossberg, the respected technology writer on the *Wall Street Journal*: 'He did what a CEO should. Hired and inspired great people, managed for the long term, not the quarter or the short-term stock price; made big bets and took big risks.'

> 'Bottom line is, I didn't return to Apple
> to make a fortune. I've been very lucky in
> my life and already have one.'
>
> STEVE JOBS

Be fair

Jobs' relationship with money was not without the odd hitch. Notably, as is so often the way, it caused more problems when there was less of it about. He did not come from a wealthy background and it would be ridiculous to think that he didn't hunger for economic stability. Not for him the hand-to-mouth existence that his parents had had to endure, or the sorts of pressures his father lived with when he received his real-estate licence just as the bottom was falling out of the market.

It was probably his desire to be economically comfortable that underpinned an alleged incident that tested his friendship with Woz. When Jobs was working at Atari, one of the company founders, Nolan Bushnell, asked Steve to come up with a game – Breakout: very much of its time, with gamers smashing a wall with a ball – in just four days. Realizing he would struggle to see the project through, Jobs drafted in Woz to help. He shared his $700 fee with Woz, splitting it straight down the middle, just as the two had shared the profits of their 'blue box' escapade. But according to a history of Atari published several years later, Bushnell was so pleased with the finished product that he gave Jobs a $5,000 bonus, none of which found its way to Woz. The story got under Woz's skin when it emerged, even though both men were worth millions by that point. Jobs remained touchy about the subject for the rest of his life. If true, it suggests that Jobs could be as fallible to the lure of money as anyone else.

Don't sell yourself short

Financial fallibility might have changed Jobs' life for much the worse if he had seen through an ill-conceived deal ahead of the release of the Apple II. As he sought additional investors to supply funding during the development of Apple II, the company drew the attention of Commodore executives. Commodore was then renowned as a producer of calculators and was moving into the computer market. Seeing Apple's potential, they made an offer for the company. Jobs put a price of $100,000 on the business, as well as stipulating that he and Woz be kept on at a salary of $36,000 each per year.

In the end Commodore's management backed out, but Jobs had tempted fate – and possibly only just survived the experience because he got a little too greedy. His behaviour also raised tensions with Woz's father, who felt, not without reason, that his son was the company's vital cog. Without Woz, he argued, there was no Apple I or II and nothing for Jobs to sell. Woz himself was more circumspect, remembering that he might have given his innovations away for free had Jobs not stepped in to protect them.

Share and share alike

There were further stresses to come on the back of Apple's initial public share offering in 1980. The IPO on 12 December that year was one of the largest in decades, with over forty employees becoming millionaires overnight. Jobs' 15 per cent holding alone was valued at a cool $220 million. But the offering also brought to light some mystifying disparities in the shareholdings of certain employees.

Such prominent figures and early committers as Bill Fernandez, Daniel Kottke and Chris Espinosa had none. Meanwhile, others who had relatively minor roles by comparison received shares as part of their remuneration package and got very rich. To some, it seemed as if the louder you shouted the more likely you were to get stock, while those who quietly got on with their business missed out. One employee sought to resolve the perceived injustice against Kottke by volunteering to double any gift of shares that Jobs made to Kottke. Jobs agreed to the deal – before adding that he would give him zero.

Apple's flotation on the stock exchange was an eye-opening experience for all. Of course, the company relied on the influx of finance to continue its stellar growth. But it also highlighted the tensions that can arise when there's big money swilling about.

Woz certainly found life working for a technology behemoth unsettling. The influx of shareholder money undoubtedly represented a fork in the road, marking an end to the period that had begun with the establishment of Apple in the Jobs family home.

For Wozniak, it seemed to coincide with a time when some of the fun drained out of the project. For Jobs, who would never again need to worry about his personal finances, it focused his mind on the fact that money wasn't everything and opened up new avenues. As he would later explain, the quest to do amazing things became his raison d'être: 'It's not just the accomplishment of something incredible. It's the actual doing of something incredible, day in and day out, getting the chance to participate in something really incredible.'

Watch your bottom line

As a gauge of good governance, the bottom line necessarily continued to be of crucial importance to Jobs after the flotation. Nor was he suddenly immune to the attractions of money. When he returned to Apple in the late 1990s, it was widely reported that he initially took a salary of only a dollar a year (50 cents for showing up and the rest performance-based, he would joke), along with a single company share and healthcare options. It was a gesture designed to show that he was back to make Apple great, not to consolidate his personal fortune.

However, he would subsequently negotiate a remuneration package that gave him a personal jet worth well over $80 million, as well as extensive stock options valued in the hundreds of millions. Given the success he oversaw, few shareholders ever begrudged Jobs his rewards but it would be over-romantic to suggest that money no longer mattered to him. Nor was he much of a philanthropist, unlike his great commercial nemesis, Bill Gates. Though he once set up a foundation, Jobs subsequently closed it, and during his second tenure at Apple he put an end to various of its philanthropic undertakings.

Nonetheless, Jobs bought an infectious energy and intensity to his work long after any personal economic imperative existed. Ironically, it was not until he had more money than he knew how to spend that Jobs truly became its master.

Don't Sideline Design

'Be a yardstick of quality. Some
people aren't used to an environment
where excellence is expected.'

STEVE JOBS

Jobs could never understand why so many people considered design to be nothing more than about the veneer, a product's final finish. He once said: 'Design is the fundamental soul of a man-made creation that ends up expressing itself in successive outer layers of the product or service.' After the runaway success of Apple II, the Apple III – released in 1980 and designed for the office market – was nothing short of a damp squib. Where Woz had previously been in virtual sole control of the technical side of the company's operations, Apple was now a big beast and everyone wanted their say in the development of the Apple III. Prominent among them was Jobs, who put many noses out of joint – see How Not to Manage Relationships (page 96) – and made a series of questionable decisions. Intent on making the III a thing of beauty, he, for instance, demanded the use of a casing that was too small for the task, causing myriad technical problems.

Jobs was also working on Project Lisa and had big ambitions for it. He wanted to use this model to incorporate lots of the technology he had first seen on his Xerox PARC tour. This was also the project on which Jobs first spurred on the workforce by urging them to 'make a dent in the universe'. But this was a trying period for Apple: there was the suspicion that the Apple III had been seriously compromised by overbearing and interfering management, not least by Jobs. The company needed Lisa to be a hit and so the pressure to ensure the same mistakes were not made again was intense. Mike Scott made the decision effectively to sideline Jobs from Lisa.

A disgruntled Jobs, whose role at the time was perhaps too loosely defined, set his sights – as we have already seen – on the far lower-profile Macintosh project. The Macintosh was intended as a relatively inexpensive computer for the ordinary man or woman on the street. This was in reality the first time that Jobs had a project of his own, with relatively free reign to do as he pleased. As such, it provides us with an excellent insight into how he believed a product should be designed.

Be practical

At the very heart of Jobs' philosophy was the idea that design was not just about how a product looks but about how it works, too. In a world where 'good design' is often understood as how pretty something is, for Jobs it was as much about usability as it was about aesthetics. It was all part of the same equation.

He also saw the intrinsic link between design and innovation. Innovation is not merely about having a great idea but also about executing that idea brilliantly – a message that a good many of the world's 'blue sky thinkers' would do well to take on board. Having a great idea is one thing, but designing a great way to put it into practice was what captured the imagination of Steve Jobs.

Keep it simple

Jobs believed that most great design was rooted in simplicity. Picasso spoke of how it took him a lifetime to learn to paint like a child. Jobs had a similar attitude to simplicity of design, believing that great simple design was the result of painstaking experimentation, testing, tweaking and improving. For him, complex design suggested a fundamental failure somewhere along the way. He expanded on this in an analysis of the problem-solving process. Most problems, he argued, initially look as if they should have a simple answer. Then, as you delve deeper, you realize that there are layers of complexity you hadn't been aware of; inevitably your solutions get more convoluted and complex. Ultimately you must find a solution that deals with all these complexities but which is itself simple.

Such was Jobs' dream for the Mac. Here was a product to be developed by a team of extraordinary minds intent on pushing back the boundaries. Their remit was to explore the most cutting-edge technologies and to imagine how they could be used to do amazing things. They were to find a way to put it all into a machine that an ordinary person could use to do previously unimaginable things. The Mac team would complete this design journey with panache.

Be a perfectionist

The computer that the Mac team came up with was sleek, even sexy, by the standards of the time, moving away from the straight lines and sharp points that had hitherto dominated the technology aesthetic. Then there was the new 3½-inch disk drive, much neater than what had preceded it, and practical, too, since floppy disks could now be carried around in a shirt pocket. To mention nothing of the delights on offer once the computer was switched on, from the unprecedented graphic interface to the mouse and the elegant word-processing software.

But design was and remains an inexact science, and even as the Mac came together Jobs was still learning. There are those who argue that some of his decisions were eccentric. For instance, his reluctance to incorporate a noisy fan into the machine meant that compromises were made on memory, with the risk of component failure also increased. In addition, he loathed machines with what he regarded as an excess of slots for additional hardware, regularly battling engineers (including Woz) who wanted to give buyers every opportunity to plug in extras. Other choices were controversial at the time but seem less so with the benefit of hindsight. Notably, he removed the cursor arrows from the Mac's keyboard so as to force the user to employ the mouse. Many an eyebrow was raised – but given the dominance of the mouse in the life of a modern IT user, who's to say that Jobs didn't make the right decision in the long run?

Remember: there's no such thing as a bad idea

At Jobs' memorial service in 2011, Jonathan Ive, his trusted design mastermind during his second spell with Apple, provided an insight into how Jobs went about the design process. He reported how Jobs was happy to put out ideas for debate during brainstorming meetings. Some, Ive said, were 'dopey' and 'truly dreadful' – but all of those were worth it for the arrival of those brainwaves that 'took the air from the room … bold, crazy, magnificent ideas, or quiet simple ones which, in their subtlety, their detail, were utterly profound'.

Evolve, iterate, improve

Jobs had given Ive unprecedented freedom with the iMac and between them they came up with a machine that – with its sensual triangular form and its see-through casing – was unlike anything else on the market. Going on sale in 1998, it became the fastest-selling product in Apple's history. Over the next few years would come the iPod, iBook, iPad and iPhone, each aesthetically pleasing, each offering a simple user experience and each harnessing new technologies to solve problems. Even Apple's packaging reflects

Jobs' design principles: simplicity, practicality and a delight to encounter. Just ask anyone who's popped a brand new iPod out of its box.

In design terms, Jobs didn't see himself as an inventor as much as a discoverer. On one occasion he was in conversation with Dr Land of Polaroid fame and conceded that he felt that the Mac had always been there, just waiting for him to come along and uncover it. The technology sector is, by definition, constantly dealing with complex problems. Jobs built his success on taking that complexity, mastering it, simplifying it for the public and selling it to them in a beautiful form. His design instincts might not have been infallible, but the legacy of the products he left behind finds overwhelmingly in his favour.

At the beginning of the 2000s, the music industry was in a state of flux. The record companies that had ruled over it – for better and worse – for a century or more were being squeezed by the arrival of cheap, easy-to-pirate digital technology. CDs that had dominated the music retail market since supplanting vinyl and tape in the late 1980s were themselves being superseded. Young computer enthusiasts with scant regard for intellectual property seemed set to take over the entire business. Then the iPod arrived into this auditory Wild West and everything changed.

When it was unveiled in late 2001, the iPod was neither the first nor the cheapest MP3 player on the market. Nonetheless, it became the must-have gadget for any self-respecting muso in the opening years of the century. So what was it that made the iPod feel so special? The answer can be given in two words: design brilliance.

The development of the iPod began in earnest when Jobs put Jon Rubenstein in charge of the project. He assembled a crack team including engineers Michael Dhuey and Tony Fadell and

British-born designer Jonathan Ive. Within just a year, the iPod was available for sale. It serves as a classic case study of what Apple under Jobs did so brilliantly.

One of the initial breakthroughs came when Rubenstein was made aware of a miniature but highly powerful disk drive that Japanese technology giants Toshiba had developed. Seeing that nobody seemed sure of how to make practical use of it, Rubenstein bought up the exclusive rights for Apple. Here was the engine that would power the machine.

Ive, meanwhile, got to work on the new project's look, feel and usability. He had joined Apple in 1992, working his way up the corporate ladder with inspirational work on several landmark Apple machines, including the visually stunning iMac. In common with Jobs, he approached every design project with the aim of producing something simple and uncluttered. As it happened, the technology inside the iPod lent itself to his sleeker-than-a-pack-of-cards design.

Hierarchical menus allowed the user to search their music collection in a variety of ways, including by artist, album and genre. Then there was the click wheel, that revolutionary and elegant wheel flush on the front of the device that let the owner search and make musical selections with unprecedented speed, as well as to play, rewind, fast-forward and adjust the volume. If any one aspect of any single Apple invention epitomizes the philosophy of simplicity as the ultimate sophistication, it is surely the click wheel.

As for colour, Ive wondered: what could be more simple and minimalist than pure white? He adopted it for the headphones, too. Of course, there were sceptics who doubted his choice – but it helped to make the product instantly recognizable around the world. Ive kept a keen eye on the aesthetics of every element of the product, down to packaging. Each iPod's serial number was etched into its fabric to avoid the need for any unsightly stickers, and neat clips instead of ugly wire ties kept the machine secure in its box. In such detail is greatness to be found.

Credit for the name iPod is believed to rest with a freelance copyrighter, Vinnie Chicco, who was employed to come up with ways to get the public on board with the new gadget. Jobs had been speaking in terms of the Mac as a hub for other devices. That put Chicco in mind of the famous line from *2001: A Space Odyssey*: 'Open the pod bay door, Hal!' With the simple addition of the Apple-classic 'i-' prefix, the iPod was with us. As luck would have it, Apple had already registered the name in relation to kiosks for public internet use, but the iPod team did not know this at the time. This offers perhaps another lesson: sometimes you can put in a lot of hard work and then serendipity will sweep in to play its part.

According to Ive, the genesis of the iPod came about not as the result of individual flashes of genius but by an arduous process of consultation between designers, engineers and manufacturers, leading to incessant tweaking and refining. Though modesty may play some part in his appraisal, it does smack of the Apple way.

Finally, there was a masterful product slogan that said everything that needed to be said, at the same time as capturing the imagination and opening up a world of possibilities: '1,000 songs in your pocket.'

'Steve, thank you for being a mentor and a friend. Thanks for showing that what you can build can change the world.'

MARK ZUCKERBERG

Sell the
Dream

'Click. Boom. Amazing!'

STEVE JOBS

Few companies have been as successful as Apple in breaking free of normal corporate expectations to become a purveyor of dreams. Sometimes it seems that Apple does not so much have customers as believers, all investing in the promise of a better lifestyle. It is a culture that has been nurtured by almost three decades of cunning and inspired advertising.

The company's breakthrough advert for the Macintosh, which broadcast in a break during the 1984 Super Bowl, is highly instructive of the philosophy it has always brought to its advertising.

- Buying advertising during the Super Bowl is expensive and not undertaken lightly. Here was a clear message that Apple meant serious business.

- The Super Bowl is just about the most watched event on American television; by appealing to such a broad audience, Apple was declaring that it had products for everyone, not just for a select band of computer nerds. This was technology for the mass market like never before.

ⓓ The advert was a take on George Orwell's dystopian *Nineteen Eighty-Four*. Directed by Hollywood stalwart Ridley Scott, it played like a mini feature film and spoke not so much of product functionality but of style and lifestyle choices – setting the tone for countless future campaigns.

ⓓ In the film an 'Everywoman' heroine runs through an Orwellian landscape brandishing a stylized picture of a Macintosh before smashing a representation of Big Brother. The slogan at the end tells us that, with the introduction of the Macintosh, 'you'll see why 1984 won't be like "1984".' And so Apple aligns itself with the rebel, the freedom-fighter, the person in search of a better future – all at the same time as having a pop at its biggest commercial rival of the time, IBM (the implicit Big Brother).

But not every campaign was as successful. The 1985 follow-up Super Bowl ad depicted corporate computer users as lemmings. Presumably intended as a comment on the sorts of people who didn't already buy Apples, it missed the mark. One could hardly imagine Pepsi depicting Coke-drinkers as sheep … an insult unlikely to persuade them to change their brand loyalty.

Rivalling *1984* as the most famous of all Apple advertising campaigns, the 'Think Different' campaign that ran from 1997 to 2002 continued the theme of challenging the status quo. Apple users, the campaign implied, refuse to be constrained by the boundaries of 'the norm'. Into the twenty-first century, the company focused its attention on winning customers from its chief competitor, Microsoft. Thus was born the 'Switch' campaign that hammered home the idea that to make 'the switch' was to take control of one's future and open up myriad new opportunities.

This idea of asserting our own individuality by buying into Apple has even allowed for a minimal focus on the company brand in several campaigns. The artwork for the iPod advertising campaign, for instance, featuring silhouetted figures enjoying their music in a way that made you want to seize an earbud for yourself, became instantly iconic and immediately recognizable as Apple. Often Apple advertising tells us little about the functionality of a product or even its price. Instead, it gives us a hint of how good it might feel to own one.

As we saw in the section 'Jobs' Heroes' (page 45), the 'Think Different' campaign aligned Apple with a host of boundary-pushers and 'outsider heroes'. Though none of them were particularly noted as Apple-owners, the clear suggestion was that Einstein would surely have crafted his Theory of Relativity on a Mac and Gandhi would have led his people to freedom to the soundtrack from an iPod, if only they had been available.

In a bid to head off accusations that Apple was exploiting the images of any of these global icons, all the people featured (or their estates if they were deceased) were promised money and computer equipment to be donated to the charities of their choice. The campaign was of crucial importance in re-establishing the company's countercultural credentials after a decade in which they had been gradually whittled away. The text of the TV advert also serves as a fine encapsulation of Apple's – and, specifically, Jobs' – philosophy. Here it is in full:

Here's to the crazy ones. The misfits,
the rebels, the troublemakers. The round
pegs in the square holes. The ones
who see things differently.
They're not fond of rules. And they have
no respect for the status quo. You can
quote them, disagree with them, glorify or
vilify them. About the only thing you can't do
is ignore them. Because they change things.
They push the human race forward.
While some may see them as the
crazy ones, we see genius. Because the
people who are crazy enough to think
they can change the world are
the ones who do.

(Script by TBWA/Chiat/Day for Apple)

Build a Community of Customers

'Most people have no concept of how an automatic transmission works, yet they know how to drive a car. You don't have to study physics to understand the laws of motion to drive a car. You don't have to understand any of this stuff to use a Macintosh.'

STEVE JOBS

Reward loyalty

One of the great skills of Jobs' Apple was to allow its customers to feel like free thinkers at the same time as being part of a community of similarly liberal, creative and forward-looking individuals. Best of all, membership was guaranteed by simply handing over your money in return for a sleek piece of technological innovation.

From the earliest Apple days it was evident to Jobs that the company's success would come from securing long-term markets, not from being content with one-off sales. While he may have dreamed of providing computers for every individual in the land during his first stint at Apple, he had the sense to realize quickly that IBM was likely to dominate the office environment, at least in the short- to mid-term. That said, he identified the educational market as still up for grabs and made a concerted play for it: here was a ready-made community to bring into the Apple fold. The company established a devoted Education Foundation, making donations to teachers and educational software developers. Apple donated computers to schools and found a route into the college market, too – to this day, there is a student discount on many Apple products. In this way, many of those who had their introductions to computers at school or college became, and remained, fans of the business. Give me the boy and I'll show you the man. Catch 'em young and you have a customer for life.

Nonetheless, Jobs always laughed off any suggestion that there was anything like a 'Church of Mac', although he did admit that the company benefitted from extraordinary customer loyalty. For some, the world remains divided between those who are 'Apple people' and those who are not. Jobs, predictably, put it down to the fact that the products were great and that consumers appreciated the fact that Apple had thought through and headed off any potential problems.

Deal in lifestyle choices

Advertising inevitably had a large part to play in fostering this extraordinary loyalty, from the urgings to 'Think Different' to the artfully composed lists of heroic boundary-breakers and the timeless elegance of the iPod-wearing silhouette. Such campaigns are as much about lifestyle choices – about choosing what sort of person you want to be – as about the products themselves. But communities are not in the end created by advertisers. They need to grow organically. From the early days when Jobs and Woz attended computer club meetings in garages in the Santa Clara Valley, there was a social aspect to the Apple culture.

Their ultimate expression is in the Macworld Conventions that began in 1985, a veritable Apple-themed carnival where the trade, customers, commentators and enthusiasts gather to celebrate and debate the company's latest output. They were also often the platform from which Jobs would introduce the latest products, becoming events that reached the front pages not just of the world's IT titles but of the newspapers, too, as well as TV, radio and the internet. To attend felt like being at the scene of history being made; to watch Jobs was to see a master communicator in action.

Under Jobs, Apple achieved what many businesses strive and fail to do: it developed an environment in which buying one of its products said something about the customer as a person. And that's why so many people stay in the gang once they've joined.

> 'Thanks for the tools, the
> inspiration, the possibilities …'
>
> TRENT REZNOR

Go for the
Big Bang

'This is landmark stuff.
I can't overestimate it!'

STEVE JOBS

In 2003, Jobs told members of the Harvard Business School: 'I understand the appeal of a slow burn, but personally I'm a big-bang guy.' Among the numerous strings to his bow, he was among the most accomplished salesmen of our time. He knew he had great products to tout and he knew how to tout great.

This was most clearly seen in the higHProfile product launches he handled personally. Andy Hertzfeld, one of the developers of the original Macintosh, has highlighted something he refers to as the 'reality distortion field' – a phrase said to derive from *Star Trek* and used to describe the way in which Steve Jobs was able to bring an audience on board with even the most extraordinary ideas through a combination of bravado, marketing skill, persistence and good old-fashioned charm. It is true that Jobs' product announcement presentations captured the imagination of the world's media like no one else's. So what did Jobs do that made him such an impressive presenter?

Don't just tell: inspire

The business presentation is all too often a dry and dull affair, centred on product specifications and sales forecasts. Jobs included all the science stuff and the figures, too, but he did his utmost to keep it interesting. If he considered something 'awesome' he'd say so. This was because he was a salesman not simply of functional products but of aspiration. Consider his words when introducing the iPod: 'In our own small way we're going to make the world a better place.'

Create a common enemy

Jobs had a gift for making us all feel as if only his products could get us out of a regressive mess of somebody else's making. Sometimes the 'enemy' was a rival company that he would imply was holding the consumer back – notably IBM in Apple's early days and Microsoft latterly. But just as often he highlighted a problem in need of solving as the villain of the piece: until the evolution of the iPod, how many of us realized that being able to carry only a thousand songs on a tiny gadget was holding us back, and that what we really needed was to be able to carry 5,000 or 40,000 tracks?

KISS

Kelly Johnson, legendary boss of the Lockheed Skunk Works, reputedly came up with this acronym, short for 'Keep it simple, stupid'. And Jobs did just that. Here was a man who sketched out his presentations not on his Mac but with pen and paper. He used language that spoke to the ordinary man on the street, not to the brain-boxes in his research departments. Acronyms and jargon might have been fine for a high-level meeting but not for a general presentation. And if he put a number into a presentation, he would be sure to explain it. On one memorable occasion, for instance, he told his audience that iPhone sales had hit 4 million, then went on to explain that this equated to sales of 20,000 a day. Likewise, during his 2007 Macworld keynote speech, he said: 'We are selling over five million songs a day now. Isn't that unbelievable? That's fifty-eight songs every second of every minute of every hour of every day.'

In such a way the figure was contextualized and made much more meaningful.

Don't overwhelm the audience

Jobs' presentations could be lengthy – regularly running to an hour and a half – but he would break up his monologue at regular intervals through the use of such tools as short films or guest interviews. He also laid out to his audience at the beginning of each presentation exactly what he would be talking about so that they knew what to expect. He would then point out the beginnings and ends of each section to provide further clarity. Similarly, his visuals were never of the complex pie-chart sort favoured by some business leaders, but rather tended towards simple but impactful images with little additional wording. He also made sure to punctuate his presentations with phrases and slogans short enough to find their way into the listeners' consciousness, into headlines and into the Twittersphere.

Leave them amazed

Jobs undoubtedly had a theatrical bent and loved the grand gesture. At the introduction of the MacBook

Air, for instance, he produced the super-thin product from a plain manila envelope as his audience gasped in amazement. He even created his own catchphrase, preceding major announcements with a Columbo-esque: 'Oh, and one more thing …' There's nothing wrong with being a showman when you've got something to sell, and such gestures will be what make the papers or get talked about around the water cooler the next day.

Practice makes perfect

Like all great performers, Jobs rehearsed to within an inch of his life so that when he went out in front of an audience he could talk as if the words had just formed in his head. (And for those of a nervous disposition, it is reassuring to know that he suffered chronically from nerves before making a big address.) It is said that he would spend up to two days before a major presentation rehearsing aloud and ensuring every detail was in place. James Brown was often called the hardest working man in show business. Jobs was the hardest working man in Silicon Valley.

Once a straggly, long-haired, ripped-denim, bare-footed hippie, by the late 1970s Jobs had made his first millions and was instead sporting smart handmade suits finished off, if the mood took him, with a bowtie. But neither of these extremes of apparel lasted. Jobs instead became synonymous with a certain look comprising signature black turtleneck, blue jeans and a pair of New Balance sneakers.

While he cut a striking figure at all those product launches, the look could not be called cool, hailing direct from the Dad School of Fashion. Yet somehow he pulled it off, to such an extent that, in the days and weeks after his death, St Croix Collections – reputedly Jobs' favourite make of turtleneck – reported a huge spike in sales. Jobs apparently bought about two dozen of the sweaters, priced at $175 each, every year.

The fact is that, while the look may not have oozed catwalk finesse, it suited the man and his company, too. It was a neat look, strangely timeless, unfussy and functional. All the things that Apple is about.

There was a time, as numerous old photos

attest, when Jobs wore suits to presentations and meetings. But in the early 1980s he made a trip to one of Sony's factories in Japan, taking the opportunity to see how his friend, Akio Morita, went about managing his empire. Jobs was struck by how all the workers wore a uniform to 'bond' them. With this fresh in his mind, he approached Japanese fashion designer Issey Miyake, who had built up a reputation for using technology in his designs. Taking up Jobs' challenge, he produced a nylon jacket with detachable sleeves for the Apple workforce – but the democratic voice at Apple was strong and the workers categorically said 'no'.

Nonetheless, Jobs was convinced that he at least should have a uniform of his own – something smart but practical. Miyake came up with the turtleneck look for him and an unlikely style icon was born.

Find a Dragon
to Slay

'I have no problem with [Microsoft's]
success. I have a problem with the fact that
they just make really third-rate products.'

STEVE JOBS

At the start of this book, we looked at how Jobs enthusiastically embraced his role as an outsider. We have also seen how Apple invokes in its fans a sense of 'us' (the Apple family) and 'them' (those outside the family). Such relationships are based on oppositions. For every 'outsider' there is an 'insider'; for each 'us' a 'them'. Jobs was a subtle and skilled master at identifying an 'other', usually a faceless giant, against whom to kick. How did he do it?

⊙ In Apple's early days, it was easy. The company was a minnow, comprising just a few young, enthusiastic, clever guys trying to make it from their offices in a family garage. At this stage, there was an easily identifiable enemy in IBM. It was simple for the new kids on the block to depict it as a lumbering old giant, building fusty machines for fusty men in suits. IBM, the implicit message said, was about propping up corporate America. Apple, by contrast, was ushering free thinkers into a brave new world.

⊙ This approach reached its apotheosis in 1981 when Apple took out a full-page advert in the *Wall Street Journal* to 'celebrate' the arrival of IBM's first PC: 'Welcome IBM. Seriously. Welcome to the most exciting and important marketplace since the computer revolution began 35 years ago …' It is difficult to imagine how Apple could more successfully have made IBM look behind the times and off the pace.

⊙ By that stage, Apple could no longer claim to be the free-rolling organization it had been five years earlier. In 1982 it would enter the Fortune 500 list, that bastion of corporate giants. Yet Jobs persisted, with considerable success, at portraying IBM as the monolithic enemy. In 1984, the year of Apple's famous Super Bowl advert, Jobs even asserted that IBM wanted to wipe Apple off the face of the Earth. In its wildest dreams, maybe, but it was scarcely a credible claim. Yet that didn't matter because it preserved the 'them and us' paradigm.

⊙ Jobs kept up the theme of Apple – or at least his Mac team – as mavericks, outlaws, sailing against the tide with soundbites such as 'It's better to be a pirate than join the Navy.'

⊙ Jobs' focus on IBM for a long while was sensible. While Apple picked up plaudits and great sales, IBM nonetheless remained a powerful beast and by the mid-1980s was winning the sales battle. But there was another major player to deal with, too: Microsoft. As the dominant force in the software market, Jobs had himself a second dragon to slay.

⊙ Today, each of the companies remains huge but Apple is the biggest of them all – yet it still manages to maintain its image as the company most likely to run a Jolly Roger up the flagpole.

It is often said that you should keep your friends close and your enemies closer. The relationship between Jobs and Bill Gates, the legendary co-founder of Microsoft, was a constantly fascinating one. Both beginning their careers in the mid-1970s, they were fierce commercial rivals and had contrasting personalities. Jobs in particular was prone to making fierce attacks, both on Microsoft as a company and Gates personally. Yet a friendship, albeit a frequently grudging one, burgeoned over time, rooted in a respect for what the other did.

In truth, the two men approached their work from vastly different positions. While Jobs viewed computers as a means to emancipate individuality, Gates saw them as a tool for doing business and as a driver of commerce. Yet both realized that they could be stronger with the other's co-operation. In 1982, for instance, Jobs persuaded Microsoft – who had produced the operating system for IBM's PC – to create a spreadsheet, database and graphics program for the Mac.

However, by the following year the two were at serious odds. As Gates heralded the imminent arrival of Windows, Jobs accused him of ripping off the Mac's graphical interface. Gates is said to have responded by observing: 'I think it's more like we both had this rich neighbor named Xerox and I broke into his house to steal the TV set and found out that you had already stolen it.'

Their relationship did not become any easier as Microsoft surged ahead in terms of commercial success. It must also have been particularly galling for Jobs that Apple seemed to need Microsoft and its pivotal software, such as Word and Excel, more than Microsoft needed Apple. The two companies spent years making lawyers rich as they wrangled over patent disputes.

Jobs resorted to some fairly crude personal attacks against Gates, once declaring that he would have been a 'broader' guy 'if he had dropped acid once or gone off to an ashram when he was younger', and on another occasion telling a reporter: 'They [Microsoft] just have no taste. I don't mean that in a small way. I mean that in a big way, in the sense that they don't think of original ideas and they don't bring much culture into their products.'

But Gates would have an important role in

turning Apple around after Jobs returned to his spiritual home in 1997. With much of the industry of the opinion that the company had had its day, Microsoft bought some $150 million of Apple stock and agreed to keep producing for Macs. Jobs publicly showed his appreciation, saying: 'I think the world's a better place for it.' Yet when a giant image of Gates was beamed into that year's Macworld Convention, Apple's avid fans began an impromptu round of booing. A case of biting the hand that feeds – and indicative of the animosity that Jobs especially had stoked between them over the years.

But as time went on, both of them became able to take a broader view of their achievements (which in Gates' case includes becoming one of the world's foremost philanthropists – something that may yet prove a more important achievement than any of his work as a software designer). Theirs was, in the final reckoning, a battle with no losers. Each is considered integral to the technological revolution that has swept the world since the 1970s. Each made epic amounts of money. Each made a significant dent in the universe.

In 2007 the two sat on the same stage at the *Wall Street Journal*'s 'D: All Things Digital' conference and were notably gracious about one another. Gates said of Jobs: 'The way he goes about things is just different, and I think it's magical.' And when Jobs was nearing the end of his life, Gates visited him at his home, where they chatted for several hours about their ideas and reminisced about their careers with all their ups and downs.

After Jobs died, Gates said: 'Steve and I first met nearly thirty years ago, and have been colleagues, competitors and friends over the course of more than half our lives. The world rarely sees someone who has had the profound impact Steve has had, the effects of which will be felt for many generations to come.'

Their rivalry no doubt drove Jobs and Gates on to new heights – and it was the wider world that felt the benefit.

Roll with
the Punches

'The PC wars are over. Done.
Microsoft won a long time ago …
Get busy on the next great thing.'

STEVE JOBS

Given the long list of Jobs' achievements, it is easy to forget that he suffered some setbacks along the way that might have downed lesser characters. But every time he was thrown from his horse he got straight back in the saddle – showing remarkable psychological fortitude in the process.

Manoeuvred out of the Apple exit door in 1985, it is fair to say that the experience, above any other, knocked Jobs sideways. He would later speak about it in terms of a punch to the stomach that knocked all the wind out of him. But rather than sitting around moping – or enjoying the not-inconsiderable fruits of his labours on some desert island – he quickly decided that his life's work was not yet done and began seeking out new opportunities. It was indicative of the restless energy that powered him throughout his life.

Jobs, it should be remembered, was just thirty at the time. He told those who would listen that he knew he still had at least one more great computer in him – a rare instance of chronic underestimation on his part, as it turned out. So, having lost his first company, he promptly set up his second, a new computer firm that he called NeXT, the name itself a grand statement of intent to move forward. He also bought a little-known company that manufactured graphics gizmos and which was destined to be renamed Pixar. The seller was one George Lucas, whose *Star Wars* franchise had shaken up the world of cinema almost as much as Jobs had shaken up computing.

If Apple was always a partnership, NeXT was decidedly Jobs' firm. As such, the shackles were off: he had a hand in everything the company did. He came up with a vision of an all-singing, all-dancing computer to take the form of an elegant cube. But it soon became clear that this machine, pairing high-end performance and cutting-edge aesthetics, was going to arrive late and could not be done at a knockdown price. Even more problematically, it was entirely uncertain that there would actually be a market for it when it finally was released.

The NeXTcube was launched in 1988 with a user-unfriendly $6,500 price tag – and more if you wanted all the supplementary kit that went with it. Even with Jobs' mighty media presence and some serious financial backing, the NeXTcube would only shift a decidedly disappointing 50,000 units in the four years that followed. The bottom line just wasn't adding up and nobody needed to tell Jobs that NeXT was not the new Apple.

By 1993 the firm had got out of the hardware market altogether – even though Tim Berners-Lee used a NeXT machine to program the fundamentals of the modern World Wide Web – and was concentrating solely on software instead. Nor was Jobs' investment in Pixar looking like a good long-term bet. As the firm struggled to find a place for its undoubtedly ahead-of-the-curve software, Jobs adopted a high-risk strategy. Pixar would focus all its attentions on film animation, an industry hardly renowned for its stability. Unimpressed with the idea of overseeing the company's collapse, he showed his ruthless side, too. In return for keeping the business funded, he demanded virtually all of Pixar's stockholding.

In 1993 the *Wall Street Journal* wrote about Jobs and his 'steep fall from a very lofty perch'. At the time few would have argued, but, as Mark Twain might have said, reports of Jobs' demise were greatly exaggerated. The journey might have been getting bumpy but he was determined to stay in the saddle.

Stay at the Top

'The magic of Steve was that while others simply accepted the status quo, he saw the true potential in everything he touched and never compromised on that vision. He leaves behind an incredible family and a legacy that will continue to speak to people for years to come.'

GEORGE LUCAS

Turn Adversity into Advantage

'The cure for Apple is to innovate its
way out of its current predicament.'

STEVE JOBS

That Jobs emerged from this difficult period to enjoy a prolonged phase of success that dwarfed even the highs of his first tenure at Apple was a remarkable feat. One of the principle reasons that it happened was that he was simply brilliant at transforming adversity into advantage.

Despite the ignominy of the end of his first Apple stint, Jobs came to regard being fired (as he effectively was) as among the most formative experiences of his life. This was not least because he got to flex his management muscles at NeXT, do extraordinary things with Pixar and meet the love of his life into the bargain. Certainly, by the time he returned to Apple in 1997 he was a more rounded person than the one who had departed a dozen years earlier. So how did he become the ultimate comeback kid?

⊙ Though Jobs and Apple will be forever synonymous, it was events at Pixar that thrust him back into the big time. The key factor was a deal with Disney that saw Pixar team up with the cinema giant to work on a feature film, *Toy Story*. The groundbreaking box-office smash of 1995, it enjoyed success – both critical and commercial – that must have taken even Jobs aback. Pixar had found its niche and a conveyor belt of cinema hits began.

ⓓ Ever the businessman, as soon as he knew that *Toy Story* was going to be hot, Jobs laid out plans to float Pixar on the stock exchange – despite company accounts showing year after year of losses. It was a typically brash move but the dot.com bubble was in its infancy and technology flotations such as this were an easy sell to investors. In the immediate aftermath of the IPO, a surge in the stock price saw Jobs' holding briefly valued at over a billion dollars. Indeed, by the time of his death, Jobs was as rich from his Pixar holdings as he was from Apple. When Pixar was sold to Disney in 2006 for $7.4 billion, Jobs' share was worth about $3 billion, making him Disney's largest single shareholder.

ⓓ In the years since Jobs had been unceremoniously dumped from Apple, he had set up one computer company that by his own standards had failed to set the world on fire and had overseen the birth of a film company that was poised to do just that. It was a mixed record but he was indubitably still in the game.

▷ Apple, though, was a distinctly lesser force. The launch of Microsoft's Windows 95 package was an event that hammered home just how far behind its rivals Apple was falling. Somewhat symbolically, a few of its machines had even started catching fire as a result of faulty batteries. Apple needed someone with vision to come aboard and steer the ship. Jobs' Apple nemesis, John Sculley, had left the company in 1993 and Jobs had ominously spoken to *Fortune* magazine of the plans he had to save his wilting former company, if only someone there would have the good sense to listen to him …

▷ Thus it was hardly a surprise when he was approached to return in 1996. But he wasn't about to kiss and make up just yet. NeXT was by no means the strongest part of Jobs' CV but here was a man who could take something and sprinkle magic dust upon it. And that is exactly what he did. He persuaded Apple to buy NeXT for a cool $400 million, about eight times more than the company had ever made in sales. Almost a third of this money went into Jobs' personal treasure chest, along with a healthy dose of Apple shares. Jobs was back where he wanted to be and wealthier than ever. Not bad for a decade and more seemingly spent in the wilderness.

> 'Sometimes life hits you in the
> head with a brick. Don't lose faith.'
>
> STEVE JOBS

Know When to Tear Up the Blueprints

'The products suck! There's no sex
in them anymore!'

STEVE JOBS

In 2006, MSNBC reported Jobs as saying: 'I think if you do something and it turns out pretty good, then you should do something else wonderful, not dwell on it for too long. Just figure out what's next.'

It is a philosophy that shows itself time and again among high achievers across the spectrum of disciplines. Consider, for instance, Sir Alex Ferguson, a man whose hunger for success remains undiminished after decades at the top of his chosen field. Ferguson is arguably the most successful manager in English football history and, at the time of writing, had been in charge of Manchester United – regularly cited as both the world's richest and best-supported football club – since 1986. In an interview with *FourFourTwo* magazine in 1999, Ferguson offered this insight with which Jobs would surely have concurred: 'Winning a trophy doesn't really mean anything to me after it's gone ... At the time it's the most cherished thing. But as soon as it's over, it's soon forgotten. Well, not soon forgotten, but it evaporates. Your next step is the important one, and the mentality here is of that nature. The players are brought up, as soon as they succeed, to go for the next thing.'

This process of incessant refocusing was also touched upon by Jobs' favourite songwriter, Bob Dylan, in the song 'It's Alright, Ma (I'm Only Bleeding)': 'He not busy being born is busy dying.' Driven by this desire to keep on being relevant, Jobs became an expert at scrapping work when he thought it was going awry and going back to the drawing board. For him, doing great work was about constantly editing what he was doing, and sometimes that meant editing savagely. In his own words: 'I'm actually as proud of the things we haven't done as the things I have done. Innovation is saying "no" to a thousand things.'

Jobs' 'back to basics' credo was evident when he returned to Apple, first as an adviser to Gil Amelio, who had been put in charge of the company in 1996, and then as interim CEO from September 1997 – the interim status giving Jobs the opportunity to model himself as iCEO. Among the first tasks he undertook was to gather together the company's top figures in a bid to find out where things were going wrong. The conclusion was simple: the products that once underpinned Apple's success were no longer up to scratch. With the gloves off, Jobs went as far as to declare that they 'sucked'. He described how he had spent several weeks trying to work out why he would buy any given product over another one, only to conclude that, if he couldn't work it out, Apple's customers certainly wouldn't.

He then set about remoulding his team and trimming the staff. Next, he got rid of Apple's printer business and cut several product lines, including some notably higHProfile projects such as the Newton handheld device. It was time for Apple to focus on doing a few things really well, just like it used to, chucking out a thousand decent ideas in that quest for the one great one. Essentially, the product line would be reduced to a desktop and a laptop for each of the business and consumer markets.

No one should have been surprised that Jobs wielded his new broom quite so drastically. As early as 1985 he had told *Playboy* that, to live in a creative way, you must be prepared to take whatever you've done and whoever you were and throw them away.

'People sometimes have goals in life. Steve Jobs exceeded every goal he set himself.'

STEVE WOZNIAK

Outpace
the Curve

'For us, it's always the next dream.'

STEVE JOBS

Jobs' desire to keep reinventing was allied to a startling ability not only to spot trends but to create them, too. In 2007 he told delegates at the 'All Things Digital' conference: 'Let's go invent tomorrow rather than worrying about what happened yesterday.'

Keep moving

Determined to remain creative and, just as importantly, to maintain revenues, Jobs was always on guard against standing still. Taking the opportunity to land a few blows on Microsoft and IBM, he once attempted to explain why Apple had overtaken them. His theory was that such companies begin as innovative forces – until they achieve some sort of market domination. At that stage, he argued, the quality of product becomes a secondary concern to keeping revenues growing. And thus, he concluded, senior management becomes dominated by sales people – those with the most obvious ability to make a quick impact on sales revenues – at the expense of the designers, engineers and dreamers.

Watch your rivals

By the early 2000s, Apple needed a new shot of energy. Its Power Mac G4 Cube had not sold brilliantly and the iMac was becoming familiar. The company hungered for a product to re-establish its credentials as a 'dent-maker'. It was against this backdrop that Jobs had one of his 'Eureka' moments.

Like everyone else in the technology sector, he was acutely aware of the growing number of unregulated file-sharing websites that were springing up, feeding an audience hungry for cheap media streamed through their computers. Manufacturers were responding by fitting out their computers with decent CD and DVD software. There was also an array of MP3 players – effectively new Walkmans for the digital age. But when he took a close look at the market, Jobs became convinced that the existing competition was, in his opinion, nowhere near up to the job.

It was time for Apple to diversify. Jobs determined

that it should create the finest digital music player out there, a machine that would dominate the portable music market like Walkmans and Discmans had dominated in the 1980s and 1990s. Though the technology was already available, Jobs was intent on binding it into a device so brilliantly designed, so pleasing to use and so far beyond anything yet conceived that it would blow every other MP3 player out of the water. His plan was to take what was already there and stretch it into something better, more efficient and more beautiful.

In 2010 Jobs would say of the iPhone 4.0: 'We're not going to be the first to this party, but we're going to be the best'; he could have said exactly the same about the iPod a decade earlier. This was the classic Jobs modus operandi, reflecting a man who saw himself less as an inventor and more as a refiner. He himself would admit: 'We have always been shameless about stealing great ideas.' In this way, the iPod was born.

Look for gaps in the market

As we have already seen in 'How to Create an Instant Design Classic' (page 116), the iPod became an immediate style icon. But it was not such an instant sales success. At the time of its launch in 2001, there were only two real options for loading songs on to it: either you uploaded songs from your own CD collection or you got tracks through an illegal website. With the music industry fearing utter implosion, Jobs had his next great moment of inspiration. He approached major record labels about the prospect of making their artists' tracks available for a small fee via an Apple-run online store using existing iTunes jukebox technology. There were, of course, some major artists who decided to remain unavailable – notably the Beatles but also the likes of AC/DC – but within a week of launch, iTunes sold a million tracks. Over the next two years it sold a billion. It was, quite literally, a lifeline for the music industry. More importantly for Jobs, it was a massive success for Apple.

At thirty years old, Jobs had spoken of the 'one more great computer' he had in him. Now in his mid-forties, he had followed up the iMac with the iPod. Where people had been writing off the company a few years earlier, they now saw it as almost peerless. The Jobs-inspired second wind continued to blow. The multi-functional iPhone came to the rescue of all those people who were becoming loaded down with gadgets, its touchscreen technology something that until recently had seemed like nothing more than science fiction. 'I do not want people to think of this as a computer,' Jobs said. 'I think of it as reinventing the phone.' So the man who would be Edison outdid Edison.

And if people were at first nonplussed by the arrival of the iPad (a touchscreen tablet) in 2010, they soon came to love it for the games they could play, the music they could listen to, the websites they could surf and, not least, for the library of books they could carry. At an age where he could have been forgiven for slowing down, Jobs had done the opposite. Apple was no longer simply a leading computer manufacturer but rather the giant of the global technology sector.

How often has the fate of a burgeoning relationship rested on the content of a music collection? Since the days of vinyl, we have judged one another by the music we listen to. The arrival of the iPod merely simplified the process of appraising somebody else's tastes. So what would you have found on Jobs' playlist?

ⓟ His tastes undoubtedly reflect his roots in 1960s West Coast counterculture and hippie-dom, though other performers suggest a penchant for stadium-filling crowd-pleasers (e.g. U2, Green Day) and grown-up dinner party soundtracks (e.g. Moby, Seal).

ⓟ There was a good dose of the Beatles and the Rolling Stones, with Jobs expressing a preference for the former when pushed on the subject. Also Joan Baez, who dated Jobs for a while in the early 1980s. But his iPod was dominated by his all-time favourite artist, Bob Dylan, with some fifteen of his albums uploaded. Jobs told biographer Walter Isaacson that his favourite Dylan song of all was 'One Too Many Mornings'.

ⓟ Jobs also had a taste for some classical music. He was a particular fan of Bach's *Goldberg*

Variations, music that on one occasion provided the backdrop to an acid trip the youthful Jobs took in a wheat field. He was also a great admirer of cellist Yo-Yo Ma, once describing him, after seeing him play live, as the best argument he'd ever heard for the existence of God.

Here is a list of some of the other artists whose music pumped through those distinctive white earbuds into the ears of Steve Jobs: 10,000 Maniacs; Black Eyed Peas; Johnny Cash; Donovan; The Doors; Aretha Franklin; Grateful Dead; Jimi Hendrix; Buddy Holly; Jefferson Airplane; Janis Joplin; BB King; John Mayer; Don McLean; Joni Mitchell; The Monkees; Simon and Garfunkel; and Talking Heads.

Create the Space for Creativity

'The system is that there is no system.'

STEVE JOBS

By the time of his second spell at Apple, Jobs was undoubtedly a wiser company leader than when he had left. This was a result of the lessons he had learned at NeXT but perhaps even more so from his Pixar experience. There, with the nitty-gritty of computer animation not his forte, he knew he had people with unparalleled skills in the art form on whom he could rely, and for the first time he learned how to manage without interfering. To put it another way, he discovered he was capable of trusting others to deliver.

Jobs also demonstrated a more mature attitude to his professional relationships, even if the odd tantrum still erupted. When he imposed a raft of redundancies at Apple after his return, for instance, he undertook the process with a deal more finesse and compassion than had been evident during a similar process at Pixar five years earlier.

But Jobs always saw his businesses as collaborative efforts and would dispense high praise when he considered it deserved. In his days in charge of the Mac project, he had acknowledged that his handpicked team of technicians and designers was the driving force behind the machine. His job, he considered, was to create a space for them, insulating them from the demands of corporate life so that they could focus on the creative process.

All he asked in return was that everyone felt a duty to the team to do their best work, aware that no one individual could do it alone. He highlighted the Beatles as a good model for a collaborative company: Jobs saw the Fab Four as a group of people who kept in check each other's negative aspects and produced work greater than the sum of their parts. This was, in brief, his dream for Apple.

'Steve Jobs was the greatest inventor since Thomas Edison. He put the world at our fingertips.'

STEVEN SPIELBERG

Jobs was as aware as anybody that, if you are going to spend a lot of time and energy on hiring the best people and blending them into a winning team, you would be foolish not to invest in giving them the perfect physical environment in which to thrive. Even in the early days of Apple, Jobs strove to make the premises as conducive to professionalism and creativity as money would allow.

Since 1993, Apple's corporate headquarters has been the Apple Campus, at 1 Infinite Loop in Cupertino, California – an area with Apple associations going back to the late 1970s. Built by the Sobrato Development Company, the Campus covers some 850,000 square feet, though Apple bought up a number of other buildings throughout Cupertino to accommodate its ever-growing workforce. With large areas of landscaped greenery, and as its name suggests, the Campus feels more like a university than corporate head offices: a place for creative minds to explore their boundaries.

But the Campus was simply not big enough to cope with the expansion of the company's operations during Jobs' second tenure. He set his mind to creating Apple Campus 2, announcing plans for the new development in Cupertino in April 2006. It is of typically visionary design, with Norman Foster + Partners – the architecture firm responsible for such iconic projects as the Reichstag redevelopment in Berlin, the Millennium Bridge in London and the Capital International Airport in Beijing – commissioned to draw up the plans. What emerged was a spaceship-like, circular glass-and-metal construction that rises four storeys, big enough to house 13,000 employees and with a strong focus on environmental sustainability.

As well as office space and research and development facilities, there are to be extensive green spaces, a 1,000-seat theatre, gym facilities, an electricity-generating plant to power it all, and even an orchard – a nod to Apple's roots. For Jobs, it was simply 'the best office building in the world'. With an estimated cost of half a billion dollars, this was never a project to be rushed and, sadly, building had yet to begin by the time of Jobs' death. It is unlikely to be ready before 2016. Nonetheless, it is set to serve as a fitting monument to Jobs' vision of how a business should operate.

Know Your Customers
(But Not Too Well)

'Our belief was that if we kept putting great
products in front of customers, they would
continue to open their wallets.'

STEVE JOBS

Trust your instincts …

The old adage says that the customer is always right, but Steve Jobs' attitude to his Apple customers was a complex one. On the one hand, his entire career was geared to providing them with products so far beyond their expectations that they had never imagined they might want or need them. On the other hand, he believed that it was his duty to know more than they did about what could be done and how it could best be achieved, so he spent little time in consultation with them.

It was a philosophy echoing that of Dr Land at Polaroid, who wrote, way back in 1945: 'I believe it is pretty well established now that neither the intuition of the sales manager nor even the first reaction of the public is a reliable measure of the value of a product to the consumer. Very often the best way to find out whether something is worth making is to make it, distribute it, and then to see, after the product has been around a few years, whether it was worth the trouble.'

The market research Jobs put most faith in was what happened at the tills once a product had been launched. If the market performance was weak it was a sign that the product was wrong and there were issues to address. Similarly, he would respond to specific weaknesses identified by users. For instance, when it became evident that a significant proportion of Macs were crashing when users activated Flash, Jobs made sure that Flash was dropped from a suite of Apple products, despite a long relationship with the application's creators, Adobe.

He always remained convinced that you cannot design by focus group. He once famously noted: 'You can't just ask customers what they want and then try to give that to them. By the time you get it built, they'll want something new.' On another occasion he expanded on the subject: 'It's not about pop culture, and it's not about fooling people, and it's not about convincing people that they want something they don't. We figure out what we want. And I think we're pretty good at having the right discipline to think through whether a lot of other people are going to want it, too. That's what we get paid to do.'

For Jobs, the design process began with the end-user experience and worked backwards. It was the job of a great designer with a great imagination to envisage that experience – not the job of the consumer.

… but respect your customers

Of course, this was a strategy that inevitably failed on occasion – which is why we remember the Mac or the iPod much more vividly than we do the Lisa or the Cube – but it was also an attitude that could sometimes rile the Apple fan base. Jobs himself acknowledged that others accused him of not listening to his customers enough and admitted that it was a complaint with some validity. In 2010 an embarrassing flaw with the iPhone 4 came to light: if the device was held in a certain way, calls could be lost. Jobs, no doubt struggling with his health issues by then, famously responded to one customer complaint on the subject by describing it as nonsense and telling the correspondent not to hold the phone in that particular way. His comments were probably no more than the manifestation of a fit of pique but it did emphasize Jobs' distance from the classic 'customer is always right' ethos.

However, given the number of customers who to this day are convinced that Jobs was always right, it is difficult to believe that either the company or the consumer would have benefitted from a culture in which prospective buyers were asked for their opinion during the creative process. It is almost unimaginable that a focus group would ever have come up with something as great as the iPod or the iPhone. Much more likely is that it would have imagined something far less impressive. Thank goodness Jobs did not settle for meeting lower expectations. As he once demanded of a quizzing journalist: 'Do you think Alexander Graham Bell ever did market research ahead of inventing the telephone?'

Reimagine the Marketplace

'We're always thinking about new
markets we could enter.'

STEVE JOBS

Not content with revolutionizing the technology that was available for sale to the public, Jobs also set about redesigning the way in which it was sold. A shop is just a shop, right? Not when Jobs got on the case. The Apple Stores are symbolic of his journey from the technology geek who set out in the 1970s to build really good computers to the global figure he became in the twenty-first century, intent on changing the very nature of our relationship with technology.

During his second spell at Apple, Jobs became increasingly frustrated at the limitations he faced in physically selling the company's goods to the public. He felt that the traditional electronic retailers were not equipped to show off Apple's wares to their optimum advantage. He was convinced that punters would pay a little extra if they could see just what Apple products offered that others didn't. But the average high street or out-of-town store was simply not geared up to provide that level of customer service. Instead, consumers were generally confronted by shelf upon shelf of boxed-up products, with the price tag often proving the decisive factor in which one they chose.

Jobs' first step towards changing the physical marketplace was to strike a deal with the major retailer CompUSA, so that 15 per cent of each CompUSA store was devoted to the Mac and the software it supported. In addition, a dedicated Apple salesman was installed in-store on a part-time basis to show customers just what the Mac could do for them.

As it turned out, the experiment was but a limited success. In terms of raw sales, it did little to change Apple's underlying fortunes. Then in 2000 Jobs made a wily acquisition to his staff, bringing in Ron Johnson who had won widespread praise for turning the Target retail chain into a major and respected nationwide player. Johnson was given free rein to assemble a team of designers and retail experts to work on creating a new consumer experience for Apple customers.

Heavily investing in top-rated design and architecture firms from around the world, the result was the Apple Store – a shopping experience a million miles from the traditional computer-retailer warehouse environment. The first two branches – at Tyson's Corner, Virginia, and Glendale, California – opened their doors for business in 2001. Gone were the imposing shelves filled with boxes. In came great glass staircases, engineered Japanese steel, expensive hardwood flooring and state-of-the-art lighting. Sleek wooden tables displayed wares arranged by task: one area of the shop dealt with music, another with photography, this sector with video editing and that with gaming.

Then there was the Genius Bar: not for sales at all but rather a place where those who already owned an Apple machine could come to get it a health-check (or even just hang out with like-minded computer geeks). Later branches would also have theatres for Apple events and studios for training sessions and workshops. And when the customer was ready to buy, a roving salesman brought a pay point to the customer, rather than requiring the customer to join a queue.

The most iconic of Apple Stores, the one that sits pretty on Fifth Avenue in New York, opened in 2006. Just as fans queued through the night for the honour of being the first to buy new Apple products, so they braved the New York night to be among the first to inspect the new retail outlet. And, boy, did they like what they saw. Sales value per square metre was soon outstripping that of Manhattan shopping institution Saks by ten to one. There are now some 400 stores across four continents, and in many cities the Apple Store is a visitor destination in its own right. Ultimately, they are a reflection of their founder's belief in simple, elegant design and superb functionality. Jobs as shopkeeper had made another dent in the universe.

By the time of his death, Jobs' name was associated with well over 300 patents logged with the US Patent and Trademark Office (USPTO). Listed sometimes as the sole patent-holder and at other times as one of a team, his portfolio encompasses everything from computers and iPods to packaging and power adaptors. He even registered two patents for the design of the glass staircase synonymous with the Apple Store. But arguably the most important of all his patents – if only for the fact that it marked his arrival on the tech scene independent of Woz – was patent no. D285.687: the Mac.

This meticulous attention to patent logging reveals that Jobs never underestimated the importance of protecting his intellectual property. While he may have aligned himself with Picasso as a keen borrower of great ideas, he clearly had little desire for others to profit on the back of his own. Inevitably, he became involved in a number of patent disputes. Indeed, at the time of writing, the validity of the so-called 'Steve Jobs patent' that covers much of the touchscreen technology upon which the iPhone relies was under review by the USPTO.

Nor was every patent Jobs logged a classic. For every Mac, for instance, there was an iMac puck – the fatally flawed mouse design that never really took off. But ultimately the secret of protecting intellectual property is not waiting around to see which of your barnstorming ideas is going to turn into a money-spinning game-changer; it is about protecting your brainwaves so that you can benefit from those that ultimately reveal themselves as winners. It only takes one or two hits for the world to forget about your misses.

Establish a Work–Life Balance

'Your work is going to fill a large part of your life, and the only way to be truly satisfied is to do what you believe is great work.'

STEVE JOBS

If Jobs' work life was one marked by almost unparalleled success, his personal life was often far rockier. In a study of his psyche, it would be remiss not to spend a little time looking at how his choices affected those closest to him, both for good and bad.

The abrasiveness that filtered through in his professional life was there in his personal life, too, not least in his youth. In his later years, for instance, he would speak of his profound regret at the cold and, frankly, ungrateful farewell he paid to his parents when he embarked on his studies at Reed. Even though he knew of the sacrifices they had made for him to go there, he barely spared them a moment as he rushed through the college gates, itching to reinvent himself independent of them.

Of course, such brashness is common among the young and few of us can be too judgemental. More problematic, though, was his initial reluctance to acknowledge his first child, Lisa, born in 1978. While Lisa's mother, Chrisann Brennan, was forced to rely on social benefits in Lisa's early years, Jobs simply refused to engage as a parent. Indeed, Brennan was eventually forced to resort to DNA testing to prove her daughter's parentage.

While Jobs' treatment of his parents on his arrival at Reed may be credibly put down to the frailty of youth, such an argument stands up less well when it comes to reneging on one's duties to a child. Even after the DNA test returned a 94 per cent probability that Jobs was the father, he continued to tell reporters that there was statistical uncertainty over the paternity. Ultimately, it took a legal judgement before he started making regular payments for the child's upbringing. Jobs' reaction was particularly harsh given the rejection he himself received in early childhood, first from his natural parents and then from what were to have been his adoptive parents. Bear in mind, too, that by 1978 the Apple II had been on sale for a year and Jobs was by no means on the breadline. Thankfully, he would eventually build a relationship with Lisa.

At other phases of his life, he appeared to have a much better balance between his professional and private lives. This is most clearly illustrated by the circumstances surrounding the start of his relationship with his second wife, Laurene Powell. It was 1989 and Jobs, a self-confessed romantic, was giving an address to students at Stanford University. In the audience was Powell, an MBA student. When Jobs had finished his talk, he made his way to the car park ahead of a further function that evening. Powell saw him and came over to speak. After a short chat, he got into his car and prepared to leave but, as he later reported: 'I thought to myself, if this is my last night on earth, would I rather spend it at a meeting or with this woman?' Deciding on the latter, he got out of his car and asked her to dinner. The two married in 1991 and went on to have three children. They strove to create as normal a family life as they realistically could, though Jobs' commitments with Apple decreed that he worked extraordinarily long hours. He was perhaps not always as attentive a parent as he might have been but his children have subsequently spoken of how they realized the importance of his work.

Jobs spoke often of the need for single-mindedness, perhaps even tunnel vision, in order to achieve really major work. He was certainly wedded to Apple and to his ambitions to change the world, sometimes at the expense of his loved ones. But with age came at least a mellowing. At the time of his death, he had navigated a ten-year marriage and left a family who clearly held him in deep affection. Perhaps one of the lessons of his life is that, however hard you try, it is impossible to have it all. But after a shaky start, he came decently close.

'You know, my main reaction to this money thing is that it's humorous, all the attention to it, because it's hardly the most insightful or valuable thing that's happened to me.'

STEVE JOBS

For a man who could call upon almost unearthly amounts of wealth, Jobs famously lived a relatively normal lifestyle. His family home, for instance, was perfectly comfortable but could hardly be described as opulent. And given his taste for denim and turtlenecks, he was not a man who adorned himself with luxurious fabrics.

In the last few months of his life, however, he devoted a good part of his energies towards the design and build of a state-of-the-art yacht. It was an unusually lavish personal project, coming in at somewhere between $130 million and $200 million.

The yacht, named *Venus* after the goddess of love and beauty, was built in the Feadship shipyard at Aalsmeer in the Netherlands. Feadship, one of the great names in the world of luxury yachts, was the perfect company for the task. Established in the 1920s and with an enviable client list, in the 1990s it built a vessel for one of the other greats of modern technology, Microsoft co-founder Paul Allen.

Venus is just over seventy-nine metres in length and has a cutting-edge lightweight aluminium hull. Along its length are a series of frameless three-metre-high windows inspired by the walls of glass familiar from the Apple Stores. The lead designer, though, was legendary French architect Philippe Starck. Work on initial drawings began in 2007, with Jobs and Starck coming together for one day every six weeks to track progress and make refinements. The ethos, inevitably, was one of simplicity and minimalism. Indeed, the finished boat looks as if it has rolled straight out of the Apple workshops. On the yacht's bridge sit seven twenty-seven-inch iMacs to make sure everything on board runs just as it should.

For Jobs, keeping up work on *Venus* throughout 2011 became a way for him to defy death for a little longer. Alas, he passed away before he could enjoy relaxing on its uncluttered teak decks, but when the Jobs family unveiled the yacht to the public in October 2012 it cut a fine figure. It is a fitting toy for the man who could have had whatever he wanted but mostly chose not to. As Starck said in an interview with the BBC: 'Steve and I shared the same idea about the elegance of the minimal, the elegance of work well done.'

Steve Jobs: Imagining a Future without Himself

'We don't get a chance to do that many things, and every one should be really excellent. Because this is our life. Life is brief, and then you die, you know?'

STEVE JOBS

Steve Jobs was decidedly a long-game player. His aim was not to delight the world today only to be forgotten by next week: he wanted nothing less than to change the world forever. For a man with an eye on the future, it is little surprise that he thought much of his own mortality. In 2005, for instance, he had warned the students of Stanford that they should not waste their inevitably limited life spans by 'living someone else's life', and told them to have the courage to follow their own hearts and intuition.

He was not obviously frightened of death. He wavered in his belief in the existence of an afterlife; indeed, he even jokingly suggested that his uncertainty on the question was why he didn't like to put on-off switches on Apple products. Nonetheless, the knowledge that there would come a time when he was no longer here undoubtedly became a motivation for him to keep on keeping on while he could. He told those assembled students in 2005, two years after he received his original cancer diagnosis: 'Remembering that I'll be dead soon is the most important tool I've ever encountered to help me make the big choices in life. Because almost everything – all external expectations, all pride, all fear of embarrassment or failure – these things just fall away in the face of death.'

Just as he had started dating Laurene Powell after wondering what he should do if that were his last day on earth, he asked himself every day whether he would be happy to be doing whatever he would be doing that day if he wasn't going to see tomorrow. If the answer was consistently 'no' for any length of time, he took it as a sign that something needed to change.

Aware of his own mortality, he thought carefully about how best to future-proof his business interests when they had to face life without him. This posed (and continues to pose) a particular challenge for Apple, for Jobs was the very personification of the brand. In 2010 the results were published of a study by three academics – Herminia Ibarra, Morton Hansen and Urs Peyer – into the performance of some 2,000 company CEOs throughout the world. They looked at, among other things, company value and shareholder returns, making adjustments for the geographical location and industrial sector of each company. They named Steve Jobs as their leading CEO, reporting that he had overseen a 3,188 per cent return and a $150 billion increase in Apple's company value in the period from his return to Apple in 1997 through to September 2009.

Jobs himself never undervalued his role within the company or the importance of the CEO role in general. For instance, he was firmly of the mind that the Polaroid company was far weaker after it effectively forced out its founder, Edwin Land, in 1980 after he had spent almost five decades at the helm. Furthermore, Jobs had already witnessed Apple struggle once after he left the company in 1985. He was therefore determined to have a plan in place before departing the scene. A major component was the appointment in 2008 of Joel Podolny, Dean of the Yale Business School, to head up Apple University. The University – an under-the-radar professional development programme for the company's executives – schools its students in the company's history, its ethos, vision and working processes. In short, all the things that have made it so successful. It could be said that the University teaches how to think like Steve Jobs.

He also planned for a dignified and timely departure from day-to-day affairs at the company. His health in evident decline, he resigned as CEO on 24 August 2011, his resignation letter stating: 'I have always said if there ever came a day when I could no longer meet my duties and expectations as Apple's CEO, I would be the first to let you know. Unfortunately that day has come … I believe Apple's brightest and most innovative days are ahead of it.'

Jobs died in the company of his family on 5 October that year. He left an estate of some $7 billion. The news of his passing was met with profound sadness both by those who knew him personally and those who knew only the public figure. Spontaneous vigils were held outside his home, at Apple's Cupertino headquarters and outside Apple Stores across the globe. A low-key funeral for close friends and family was followed by a memorial service in Cupertino, an eighty-one-minute video of which (entitled 'Celebrating Steve') was uploaded to the Apple website. A stellar list of attendees included the great and the good from the worlds of business, politics and entertainment. Bill Clinton and Bill Gates rubbed shoulders with Bono, Al Gore and Joan Baez, while Norah Jones and Coldplay provided some entertainment.

And what of his legacy? Some analysts responded to Jobs' death by advising investors to sell their Apple shares. *The good times are over,* they argued. *The ringmaster is gone and the circus won't survive.* Of course, without him Apple is becoming a different beast and some wonder whether it will retain that knack for getting things so instinctively right, though it was widely reported that Jobs had left a legacy of ideas and blueprints – including television and Cloud-related products – to last for several years.

'For those of us lucky enough to get to work with him, it's been an insanely great honour.'

BILL GATES

But commercial landscapes can change. What is now historical record is that Jobs was a giant, perhaps even *the* giant, of the technology business from the 1970s until the 2010s. On his death, Apple released a statement that said: 'The world is immeasurably better because of Steve.'

He was a man who strove to make a dent in the universe. He did. And then he made another. And another. And another …

'I have looked in the mirror every morning
and asked myself: "If today were the last day of my
life, would I want to do what I am about to do today?"
And whenever the answer has been "No" for too many
days in a row, I know I need to change something.'

STEVE JOBS

Acknowledgements

In the course of writing this book, I was able to mine an extensive array of material on Steve Jobs. In terms of news media, the *Wall Street Journal*, the *New York Times*, *Time* magazine and *Fortune* magazine documented his career particularly usefully.

Walter Isaacson's *Steve Jobs: The Exclusive Biography* (Little, Brown; 2011) was an invaluable source of insights, as was Woz's own *iWoz: Computer Geek to Cult Icon: How I Invented the Personal Computer, Co-Founded Apple, and Had Fun Doing It* (W. W. Norton & Company; 2007). Other titles in a selected bibliography include George Beahm's *I, Steve: Steve Jobs In His Own Words* (Hardie Grant Books; 2011), Karen Blumenthal's *Steve Jobs: The Man Who Thought Different* (Bloomsbury Publishing; 2012) and Michael Moritz's *Return to the Little Kingdom* (Duckworth Overlook; 2009).

Also, thanks to my two editors at Michael O'Mara, Mathew Clayton, who commissioned the title, and Silvia Crompton, who saw it through to completion. Thank you, too, as ever, to Rosie.

If you enjoyed *How to Think Like Steve Jobs*, you'll love

It's elementary!

978-1-84317-953-5 in hardback format
978-1-84317-971-9 in ePub format
978-1-84317-972-6 in Mobipocket format

More exciting new titles to choose from:

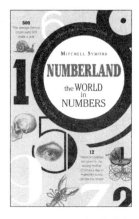

978-1-78243-060-5 in hardback format
978-1-78243-159-6 in e-book format

978-1-84317-000-1 in hardback format
978-1-78243-073-5 in ePub format
978-1-78243-072-8 in
Mobipocket format

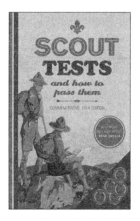

978-1-78243-143-5 in hardback format
978-1-78243-170-1 in e-book format